Reading for Today

A Sequential **1** Program for Adults

TEACHER'S EDITION

Program Authors	Jim Beers	**Program Advisors**	Sharon Darling
	Linda Ward Beech		Susan Paull
	Tara McCarthy		Lonnie Farrell
	Jo Ann Dauzat		Aryola Taylor
	Sam V. Dauzat		Adriana Figueroa
			Carol Paggi
Teacher's Edition Author	Norman Najimy		Jean Batey
			Ann Reed
Program Consultant	Donna D. Amstutz		

Steck-Vaughn Adult Education Advisory Council

Donna D. Amstutz
Asst. Project Director
Northern Area Adult Education
  Service Center
Northern Illinois University
DeKalb, Illinois

Roberta Pittman
Director, Project C3 Adult Basic
  Education
Detroit Public Schools
Detroit, Michigan

Elaine Shelton
Consultant, Competency-Based
  Adult Education
Austin, Texas

Lonnie D. Farrell
Supervisor, Adult Special Programs
Los Angeles Unified School District
Los Angeles, California

Don F. Seaman
Professor, Adult Education
College of Education
Texas A&M University
College Station, Texas

Bobbie L. Walden
Coordinator, Community Education
Alabama Department of Education
Montgomery, Alabama

Meredyth A. Leahy
Director of Continuing Education
Cabrini College
Radnor, Pennsylvania

Jane B. Sellen
Supervisor, Adult Education
Western Iowa Tech Community
  College
Sioux City, Iowa

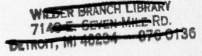

STECK-VAUGHN COMPANY
AUSTIN, TEXAS
A Division of National Education Corporation

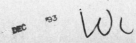

Table of Contents

TE ISBN 0-8114-1900-2

3 4 5 6 7 8 9 0   VP   90 89 88 87

STECK-VAUGHN
YOUR CHOICE
FOR A LITERACY PROGRAM!

Program components: <u>Reading for Today</u> student's books, teacher's editions, diplomas, and the accompanying <u>Communication for Today</u> workbooks.

IDEAL FOR TUTORS!

Scope and Sequenc

BOOK TITLE	SIGHT WORDS	PHONICS
1 0–1 r.l.	▶ A total of 93 function words, content words, and number words are presented, reviewed, and recycled.	▶ Letter-sound associations for initial consonants *Bb–Zz* taught in Unit 1 and reviewed in Units 2–3.

2
 	
1.0–2.0 r.l.
	▶ **Sight word pages** introduce 61 new words in *Book 2*.
	▶ **Review word pages** reinforce the 93 *Book 1* words.
		▶ Short vowels taught and reviewed through these word families:
		   1. Short *a* in *-at, -an, -ad, -and*
		   2. Short *e* in *-end, -ent, -et, -ed*
		   3. Short *o* in *-op, -ot*
		   4. Short *i* in *-in, -it*
		   5. Short *u* in *-ut, -un*
		▶ Initial consonants reviewed and recycled.

3
 	
2.0–3.0 r.l.
	▶ **Sight word pages** introduce 63 new words in *Book 3*.
	▶ **Review word pages** reinforce 84 key sight words from *Books 1–2*.
		▶ Long vowels taught and reviewed through these word families:
		   1. Long *a* in *-ake, -ay*
		   2. Long *i* in *-ine, -ight*
		   3. Long *o* in *-ope, -old*
		   4. Long *e* in *-eed, -eat*
		   5. Long *u* in *-une, -ute*
		▶ Short vowels reviewed through these word families: *-ag, -ell, -ip, -ig, -ug*
		▶ Introduced in context: *st, sh, wh, pr, dr, str, th, cl*
		▶ Initial consonants reviewed and recycled.

4
 	
3.0–4.0 r.l.
	▶ **Sight word pages** introduce 84 new words in *Book 4*.
	▶ **Review word pages** reinforce 84 key sight words from *Books 2–3*.
	▶ **Life-Skill pages** introduce 22 new words in *Book 4*.
		▶ Consonant blends taught:
		   1. *r* blends: *br, cr, dr, fr, gr, pr, str, tr*
		   2. *s* blends: *sc, sk, sm, sn, sp, st, str, su*
		   3. *l* blends: *bl, cl, fl, gl, pl, sl*
		▶ Consonant digraphs taught: *ch, sh, shr, th, wh*
		▶ Silent consonants taught: *wr, kn, gu, g*
		▶ Long vowel *i* and *e* spelled *-y* taught
		▶ Long and short vowels reviewed through word families *-ack, -ank, -ate, -ean, -ear, -eep, -eet, -ink, -ing, -ill, -ick, -ock, -ub, -y*

5 4.0–5.0 r.l.	▶ **Sight word pages** introduce 84 new words in *Book 5*. ▶ **Review word pages** reinforce 84 key sight words from *Books 3–4*. ▶ **Life-Skill pages** introduce 29 new words in *Book 5*.	▶ Vowel digraphs taught through word families: *-ain, -ame, -ie, -ice, -ue, -ew, -all, -aw* ▶ Diphthongs taught through word families: *-oil, -oy, -own, -ound* ▶ R-controlled vowels taught through word families: *-ark* and *-orn* ▶ Consonant blends and digraphs reviewed and recycled.

f Program Strands

STRUCTURAL LANGUAGE	COMPREHENSION/LIFE-COPING SKILLS
▶ Adding inflectional endings -s, -ed, -ing to known words (verbs) ▶ Adding -s to form plurals of known words (nouns)	▶ Students learn to read words, then sentences, then paragraphs. ▶ Students read to **recall facts and details** in a short story.
▶ Forming plurals with -s ▶ Adding inflectional endings -s, -ed, and -ing to verbs ▶ Forming contractions ▶ Capitalizing sentences and proper names ▶ Forming singular possessive of nouns with 's ▶ Doubling the final consonant to add -ed and -ing to verbs	▶ Students read for **facts and details** in reading selections that focus on these life-coping themes: 1. Managing money 2. Moving to find work 3. Maintaining health 4. Using leisure time 5. Coping with false arrest 6. Understanding self and others 7. Selecting a satisfying job
▶ Compound words ▶ Irregular plurals ▶ Adding -er to nouns ▶ End punctuation of sentences ▶ Irregular verbs ▶ Dropping final e to add -ed and -ing to verbs ▶ Quotation marks in dialog	▶ Students read **for facts** and **to find the main idea** of selections that focus on these life-coping themes: 1. Recognizing hidden costs to consumers 2. Rearing children 3. Promoting health care 4. Handling social relationships 5. Learning about prison programs 6. Coping with job dissatisfaction 7. Working in the performing arts
▶ Irregular verbs ▶ Prefixes re- and un- ▶ Plurals with -ies ▶ Suffixes -ly, -ful, -ness, -y ▶ Abbreviations and titles ▶ Days of the week/months of the year	▶ Students read to **find facts, main idea, sequence**, and **words in context** in selections that focus on these life-coping themes: 1. Buying with coupons 2. Helping children learn to read 3. Becoming a parent 4. Understanding others 5. Advising juvenile delinquents 6. Overcoming shyness 7. Starting a new career
▶ Word building skills reviewed: forming plurals, adding inflectional endings, adding prefixes and suffixes ▶ Adding -er and -est to adjectives to form comparatives and superlatives ▶ Writing a friendly letter ▶ Changing y to i to add -es, -ed ▶ Forming plural possessive of nouns ▶ Irregular verbs ▶ Reflexive pronouns ▶ Plurals with -es	▶ Students review learned skills: **recalling details, finding main idea, sequence, understanding words in context.** Students also **infer information** from facts given in selections that focus on these life-coping themes: 1. Buying goods on credit 2. Adapting to a new country 3. Teaching children about safety 4. Using leisure time 5. Following immigration procedures 6. Handling social relationships 7. Finding work as an artist

Author Team and Consultants

Authors

James W. Beers, Ph.D., is a professor of reading and language arts at the College of William and Mary, Williamsburg, Virginia. Jim is the coordinator of the graduate reading program and director of the Eastern Virginia Writing Project. Jim serves on the board of directors of Rita Welch Adult Skills Program at William and Mary, and on the editorial board of *The Language Experience Journal*.

Linda Ward Beech, B.A., author and educational writer, is currently tutoring adult basic education students in New York City. Linda has authored and contributed to many kinds of educational materials including magazines for reluctant readers, textbooks in language arts and spelling, dictionaries, and workbooks for low-level readers.

Tara McCarthy, M.A., professional writer and former teacher, conducts Title I inservice training workshops and has written several books for adults with low reading levels. She is a member of International Reading Association (IRA), National Council of Teachers of English (NCTE), and the Association of Curriculum Development (ASCD). Tara has coauthored numerous textbooks, learning kits, and supplementary materials for students with reading or learning disabilities.

Sam V. Dauzat, Ed.D., is professor and coordinator of teacher education at Louisiana Tech University. He is past president of the board of the North Louisiana Reading Council. Sam has directed state and federally funded workshops on adult education and has taught reading at the Adult Reading Academy at Louisiana Tech.

Jo Ann Dauzat, Ed.D., is a professor and Director of the Center for Field Services and Research at Grambling State University in Louisiana. She is past president of the board of the North Louisiana Reading Council. Jo Ann has taught reading at all levels from kindergarten through adult.

Teacher's Edition Author

Norman Najimy, M.S., is the principal of Richmond Consolidated School in Richmond, Massachusetts. He is past director of English at Pittsfield Public Schools, Pittsfield, Massachusetts. Norman has taught ABE classes in Pittsfield, Massachusetts, GED English classes for National Educational Television, and ESL classes in Beirut, Lebanon.

Program Consultant

Donna D. Amstutz, M.S. Ed., has been active in adult basic education for over 14 years. After working for the Illinois State Board of Education's Adult Education Section, she taught ABE/GED. She moved on to become a materials/curriculum specialist and conducted staff development for 30 ABE programs. During this time, she wrote *The Adult Basic Education Sourcebook: Answers to Questions Commonly Asked by ABE/GED Teachers*. She has developed curriculum for City Colleges of Chicago and administered their ABE program. Currently she is Project Director at the Education Service Center, Region II at Northern Illinois University where she provides staff development to 16 ABE programs in northwest Illinois.

Program Advisors

Lonnie Farrell, M.A., is Supervisor of Adult Special Programs for the Los Angeles Unified School District, which serves over 100,000 adult students. Lonnie's staff of teacher advisors includes **Aryola Taylor**, teacher/advisor in the central office, **Adriana Figueroa**, site coordinator of the Mid-City Adult Basic Education Center, **Carol Paggi**, site coordinator of the Southgate Adult Basic Education Center, **Jean Batey**, counselor at the Venice Adult Learning Center, and **Ann Reed**, reading teacher at Venice Adult Learning Center. This dedicated group served as advisors and reactors to each lesson in *Reading for Today*.

Sharon Darling, M.A., holds advanced degrees in counseling and educational administration. She is currently Director of the Division of Adult and Community Education of the Kentucky Department of Education. Sharon is past director of the Jefferson County Adult Reading Program (JCARP) which she developed. This program has been nationally validated by the National Diffusion Network of the U.S. Department of Education. Her career includes teaching and supervising in elementary schools and adult literacy programs.

Susan Paull, B.A., is Literacy Coordinator for the National Dissemination Project of the Jefferson County (Kentucky) Adult Reading Program (JCARP). Susan has trained over 400 teachers from 16 states to implement literacy programs based on the JCARP model. She has also written and presented the script of "Teach An Adult to Read," a volunteer training program on Kentucky Educational Television.

Field Test Sites

We gratefully acknowledge guidance from students and staff of these adult education sites for volunteering to field test *Reading for Today*.

St. Vrain Valley School District
Adult Learning Center
Longmont, Colorado

The St. Vrain Valley Adult Education Center near Denver serves 600 adults below the high school completion competency level. The year-round program is managed by Intake Specialist Lucy Stromquist. Kathy Santopietro, from this center, was chosen 1986 Teacher of the Year by the National Commission on Adult Basic Education.

Adult Learning Center
Worcester Public Schools
Worcester, Massachusetts

The Worcester Adult Learning Center is in New England's second largest city. Director Jim Jasper and a staff of 25 annually serve the needs of over 2,200 enrolled adults in the areas of ESL, ABE, and GED.

L'Anse Creuse Adult Education Program
Macomb County Jail
Mt. Clemens, Michigan

Located in a suburb of Detroit, the Macomb County Jail houses 600 inmates. Approximately 75% voluntarily take advantage of the adult learning center's 15 classes. Tim Myrand, Jail Coordinator, supervises 14 adult educators.

Seminole Community College
Adult and Continuing Education Division
Sanford, Florida

The Adult Education Division of Seminole Community College serves 25,000 students per year. Its Developmental Education Branch, headed by Marilyn Mitchell, provides ABE/GED programs for 7,000 students, and has 35 outreach centers throughout Seminole County.

Northeast Independent School District
Adult Education Program
San Antonio, Texas

This program in Texas's third largest city offers adult classes on 24 campuses and serves 1,000 students. Arline Patterson is Assistant Director of Special Programs for Community Education for Northeast.

Reading for Today: Program Overview

Reading is a complex thinking process and includes many subskills that operate simultaneously. Let's look a little closer at that statement.

The first challenge facing the beginning or impaired reader is "code breaking"; otherwise reading new words will be simply a guessing game. But recognizing words is not enough. What tutor or teacher has never seen a "word caller," reading individual words but with no understanding of their meaning? Understanding must be developed through background building, and this is the purpose of discussion, or oral language. Familiarity with English syntax is another essential subskill: reading must feel like talking, talking in print.

Reading as a Whole Act

Steck-Vaughn has created *Reading for Today* in response to this view of reading. We believe that reading is a whole act. In this sequential program, we ask the student to read units that teach and practice all subskills simultaneously. We teach reading organically, developmentally, as a growing and living thing. As students progress from unit to unit, book to book, this complex act, reading, gets easier and grows stronger.

Many Strands Build Reading Power

1. Life-Coping Themes—Real life permeates the entire program. The gripping adult themes central to each unit are of high interest; they motivate students who begin this program and compel them to stay with it.

Each unit in *Books 2-5* is developed around a high-interest adult situation, such as false arrest, moving to find work, trying to quit smoking, overcoming shyness, etc. While these themes relate to the adult competency categories identified by the Adult Performance Level research (consumer economics, job knowledge, health and safety, community resources, and government and law) their realistic, dynamic presentation is unique.

2. Sight Words—Sight vocabulary is the core of words a reader recognizes automatically. Adults usually bring a sizable sight vocabulary to your class. It's your job to make it include the Dolch 220 List: words which occur most frequently in printed material. *Reading for Today* teaches these essential Dolch words as sight words and provides repeated exposures for each one.

Adults also need to learn highly useful content words as soon as possible: *holiday, music, smoking, parents, baseball*, etc. *Reading for Today* has selected groups of useful words and teaches them as sight words. Finally, essential content words from the EDL Core Vocabulary List are chosen to round out the sight word bank.

After a sight word is introduced, the student is repeatedly exposed to that word, not just in one unit, but throughout the book and again in the following book. *Overlearning* these words is the goal, the key to confidence and success.

3. Phonics—Adults tend to learn words as wholes or as chunks that fit together; breaking words into individual speech sounds and blending them can be very difficult. Adults also need to learn quickly some basic code-breaking techniques, so *Reading for Today* uses sight words to lead the adult into phonics as soon as possible. The time-honored and highly successful *word family approach* is the main phonics tool. The student begins with a known sight word such as *can* and builds more -*an* words through initial consonant substitution. In this quick, painless way adults learn the basics of phonics. They master initial consonants in *Book 1*, short and long vowels in *Books 2* and *3*, and vowel digraphs, diphthongs, and r-controlled vowels in *Books 4* and *5*.

4. Oral Language—Adults have a wealth of knowledge and experience. Talking about an adult theme gives them confidence and helps provide a mental set for reading. An oral language strand is incorporated in each unit, and is an essential part of the unit opener and the concluding three-page story.

Oral language activities in the unit opener lead students to relate reading to their own lives and real concerns. Discussion can bring out the concepts behind the words to be learned in the unit, giving the student a head start and building a feeling of comfort and confidence.

5. Structural Language—Written English is full of oddities such as irregular plurals, irregular verbs, abbreviations, contractions, suffixes, etc. Each unit in *Books 2-5* focuses on practice of one written language skill. *Book 1* begins this strand with instruction on adding the inflectional endings -*s*, -*ed*, and -*ing* to known words.

6. Comprehension—*Reading for Today* targets the five basic comprehension skills that ABE students must use daily when they read: 1) recalling facts and details; 2) finding the main idea; 3) putting events and ideas in a sequence; 4) drawing conclusions; 5) identifying words through context clues. These comprehension skills are presented gradually in the program. Once a skill has been introduced, it is reviewed in all the later books.

Vocabulary: Controlled & Reviewed

Reading for Today helps students achieve real success because the vocabulary is carefully controlled and continually reviewed. Students learn new words at a steady pace and are never expected to guess at words not yet introduced. Constant repetition of words after their introduction builds real confidence, real mastery. Controlled vocabulary puts the students in control of their learning. They can read successfully, at last!

Pacing the Vocabulary Load

In *Book 1*, students learn consonant sounds and 93 sight words. In *Book 2*, they learn another 165 words. Each unit of *Book 2* (and each subsequent book) reviews twelve words from previous units, then introduces nine new sight words.

Two of these sight words in each unit serve as models for the phonics pages. For example, in *Book 2*, unit 2, students learn *send* and *went* as sight words on pages 16-17. Then on page 18 they use the known word *send* to learn five more -*end* words; on page 19 they use the known word *went* to learn six more -*ent* words.

You can be sure that every word in each story has been previously introduced. A master word list for each book is available at the back of each student book. Your students will achieve success because they begin with known words and move from the known to the unknown.

State-of-the-Art Research

Reading for Today is a state-of-the-art literacy program, based on the best available research and practice. An independent market research firm conducted a quantitative study of teachers of adult reading to find out what users want, use, and find successful. Teachers' responses to questionnaires show that they want sight words taught at all levels, phonics practice, real-life topics, natural language, practice in speaking and listening, a multi-level program, and teacher's editions with notes on the same page as the student's lesson. These findings have been implemented in *Reading for Today*.

The latest educational research was studied thoroughly by the authors and editors. Three pertinent points surfaced: that reading is a whole act and too much separate teaching of the subskills can be counterproductive; that phonics or breaking the code is a necessary first hurdle to be overcome; and that controlled vocabulary (combined with realistic art and photos) works for low-level readers. Again, these features are found in *Reading for Today*.

Reading for Today's research team is a select group of experienced adult education specialists who advised Steck-Vaughn at all stages of development: Donna Amstutz, Lonnie Farrell, Sharon Darling, Susan Paull, and the Steck-Vaughn Adult Advisory Council. Our author team and editors visited adult education centers to observe classes and talk with students and teachers to gain the real-life perspective of ABE teachers' needs. Finally, field test sites listed on page T-9 contribute classroom verification to *Reading for Today*.

Description of the Books

BOOK 1

This entry level book is for adults with no prior reading or writing skills, and is written on a 0-1.0 reading level. *Book 1* has two main objectives: 1) to teach students initial consonant letters and sounds, using key words and key pictures to help memorize and connect sounds and letters; 2) to teach a core of 93 of the most common sight words that all readers need to learn. These basic words include the most common nouns and verbs as well as function words such as *a, the, was, of, with, for, this,* and *you.* Because these basic words must be mastered quickly, *Reading for Today* presents them repeatedly in a variety of word groupings with interesting photo settings.

The *Book 1* words were selected by frequency of usage from the following well-known lists: the Dolch Basic Sight Vocabulary, the EDL Core Vocabularies, the Mitzel Functional Reading Word List for Adults, the Kuçera-Francis List, and the Madden-Carlson 250 Words of Highest Frequency in Our Language.

Book 1 differs from the other four books in that it contains three units: a phonics unit consisting of letter-sound associations for consonants, then a unit on sight words in short phrases such as *a big dog* or short sentences such as *A woman works*, then a unit on sight words and function words within complete sentences. Students also practice word building by adding *-s, -ed,* and *-ing* to known words. *Book 1* is illustrated with 200 photos to aid word recognition. This book concludes its 80 pages with a two-page reading selection composed entirely of words students have mastered, as a lead-in to the reading selection in unit 1 of *Book 2*.

BOOK 2

Written at the 1.0-2.0 reading level, *Book 2* begins the seven-unit structure of all subsequent books. Each unit focuses on a different life-coping theme, such as managing money in unit 1. Each unit contains these six kinds of lesson pages: (1) a unit opener on which oral language is developed as the unit theme is presented in a teaser; (2) a review words page that reinforces twelve words from a prior unit; (3) sight word pages which introduce three new words per page in sentence context; (4) phonics pages on which a short vowel sound is learned by building a word family from a known word; (5) a structural language page that teaches skills such as forming the possessive of known words; and (6) a culminating comprehension lesson—a three-page reading selection on the unit theme in which students apply all the unit skills to read words in context and answer comprehension questions.

Final review pages for all units are placed after the seventh unit. Each student book concludes with a master word list.

BOOK 3

Book 3 is written at the 2.0-3.0 reading level, and its structure is identical to *Book 2*. Students who complete *Book 2* will feel at ease with *Book 3* exercises and directions because of the similarity. Each unit in *Book 3* presents a different theme from those in *Book 2*. Phonics pages in *Book 3* introduce long vowel sounds and review short vowel sounds via word families. Comprehension skills progress from recalling details in *Book 2* to finding the main idea in *Book 3*. *Books 2* and *3* each contain 96 pages.

BOOK 4 AND BOOK 5

These two upper-level books contain all the elements of *Books 2* and *3*. *Book 4* is written at the 3.0-4.0 reading level and *Book 5* is at 4.0-5.0; both are 112-page books. These books contain two new kinds of lesson pages in addition to those in *Books 2 and 3*. (1) Comprehension skill page: Following the reading selection, this page asks students questions about the story and gives helpful hints on how to find the main idea or other comprehension skill featured. (2) Life-coping skill page: The final page of each unit is a special feature concerned with real-life materials that adults must be able to read to effectively cope: reading a prescription label, a telephone book list, a schedule, etc. Students discuss the item and answer questions about its content, thereby applying reading skills to everyday situations.

Related Material

A diploma that is suitable for framing is available for each student who completes a book in the program. The diploma states that the student has successfully completed one level and has gained the skill proficiency to progress to the next level.

Communication for Today is a series of five practice workbooks correlated to *Reading for Today* for ABE students who need more practice to master all the reading skills in *Reading for Today*.

To the Tutor

This program was developed for easy use by volunteer tutors as well as certified teachers. As a tutor, you can develop the "how to" skills of teaching reading by using the introductory pages and the teaching notes on each page. *Reading for Today* has a solid sequence and carefully planned lessons; you need not be a trained teacher or reading expert to help students.

Your student needs your patience, understanding, and encouragement, however, while learning new and difficult skills. These essential qualities are as important to your student as the teaching techniques you use. Tutors will build rapport with students by listening to their problems, encouraging their efforts, and showing patience and understanding when students make mistakes. Adult students need to build feelings of self-confidence and success as a necessary part of learning to read.

Tutor Expectations

As a tutor you naturally will expect to see progress and growth in your student. However, your expectations must be realistic. Progress with adults is sometimes measured inch by inch. If your expectations are too high and you become disappointed in your student, the student in turn will become discouraged and frustrated. Be aware of the small steps your student makes, and treat each step as progress toward the goal of reading. When a student recognizes a sight word that he or she did not recognize yesterday, this is progress; say so. If a student can put together what he or she already knows to sound out a new word, this is progress; say so.

Profile of the Adult Learner

The *Reading for Today* series is designed specifically for the adult student. The content, design, and illustration of these books have all been developed to attract and hold the interest of adults. Before using these books with your student, consider the ways in which adult learners are different from children.

GOAL-ORIENTED—The adult who enters a reading program usually has a specific reason: to get a certain job or promotion, to get a driver's license, to read to one's children. Statistically many adults quit after about two weeks in a literacy course because the long-term goal is so far off. Ask your student to tell you his or her short-term goals. Help your student have a feeling of success every day.

COMPETENT—Adult students have been functioning in the adult world for years. They have jobs, hobbies, friends, and families. They have achieved all this without one of the survival skills: reading. They are mature people who are used to being treated as such.

RESPONSIBLE—The adult learner, unlike the child or teenager, has many responsibilities in addition to schoolwork: earning a living, taking care of a home, specific personal problems. As a result, many students have little time to review and absorb large amounts of material at one time.

INITIALLY MOTIVATED—Adult students are usually highly motivated when they enter a reading program. However, this motivation may lessen as time passes and their other responsibilities affect the time and energy they can devote to reading. Be prepared for that.

Part of the tutor/teacher's job is to keep the student's motivation high. Many adult students see themselves as failures. Encourage feelings of success by placing your student in the appropriate level in the program, giving recognition for each small success, and giving positive feedback.

Discussion Techniques

Structure and guide any discussion so it does not become idle conversation. Use discussion to clarify the relationship between the lesson and the student's life.

If you have a group, be aware of students who dominate the discussion, and those who hesitate to participate. Moderate the first and encourage the second.

Questioning Strategies

Because adult learners are especially sensitive to failure, questioning an adult requires special skill. The kinds of questions you ask and how you ask them can promote feelings of success or failure. Follow these guidelines as you pose questions to your student:

a. If the student does not understand the question, rephrase it.

b. If the student gives an incorrect answer, don't dismiss it abruptly. See if the answer is based on a misunderstanding of the question.

c. If a student can't respond, don't focus too long on that question. Give words of encouragement and later ask an easier question.

Below is a sample dialog based on the paragraphs on page 72 of *Book 1*. Notice the techniques that promote a feeling of success.

> **T:** Where do the man and the speaker go after work? (simple recall question)
> **S:** To the home of a sick family.
> **T:** Why do they go there?
> **S:** To visit.
> **T:** That's true. Let's reread the second paragraph and see if there is another reason. (Read, then rephrase the question). What does the man have for them?
> **S:** He has food.
> **T:** That's right. He is bringing food to the sick family.

Building a Scale of Questions

To assure that you ask thoughtful questions, think of ranking the difficulty of your questions on three levels, such as recall, comprehension, and interpretation. **Recall** questions are simple factual questions (who, what, when, where). **Comprehension** questions require that the student understand a statement. **Interpretation** questions require the student to see beyond the facts to compare and contrast details, or to apply facts to a different situation.

The following sample questions illustrate these three levels of questioning, based on the story in *Book 2*, unit 3.

1. Recall:
> **T:** In the story, what habit was Van trying to break?
> **S:** Smoking.

2. Comprehension:
> **T:** Tell in your own words what Van meant when he told Pat "Smoking was a ticket to feeling in."
> **S:** Answers will vary, but the student should express the idea that Van smoked to feel that he was part of a group.

3. Interpretation:
> **T:** Van says that they are going to ban smoking where he works. Suppose you are Van's boss. Give reasons why this might happen.
> **S:** Answers will vary. The student could list: decreased fire hazards/fire insurance rates; decreased sick leave for smoking-related illnesses; a cleaner, healthier environment in which to breathe; etc.

Book 1 Teaching Notes

Unit 1

Consonant Pages 5–9, 11–15

1. Write the letter *b* on the board, and have the student tell you the letter name. Tell the student that *b* stands for the sound heard at the beginning of *ball* and *belt*.
2. Ask the student to (a.) look at the small picture next to the letters *B b*, and name the object; (b.) read the word and name the letter at the beginning of *bed*; (c.) name other words that start with *b*.

3. Read the directions aloud. Have the student study the photo. Ask the student to name the objects or actions in the photo. Write the answers on the board, read the words aloud, and have the student repeat them after you.
4. Ask the student to name the letter that *bed* starts with, and to write it in the blank on the page.

Review Pages 10, 16

1. Write the key words from prior pages on the board. Read the words, and have the student read after you. Go over the list until the student can read it unassisted. Then ask the student to name other words that start with consonants *b–m*.

2. Discuss the photo in *A*. Guide the student to complete the exercise independently.
3. In *B*, the student must apply the beginning sounds learned to new words. The student will name each object and write the beginning letter.

Unit 2

Sight Word Pages 18–21, 24–27, 30–33, 36–41

1. Teach each 2-page sight word section in unit 2 as one lesson.
2. Have the student discuss the photo on the left-hand page, and identify the objects and actions.
3. Read the new words aloud. Have the student repeat the words. Ask for sentences using the words.

4. The photo is labeled with the new words. Help the student write each word next to the correct number in *B*.
5. Begin the right-hand page by reading the 5 new words aloud. Have the student repeat after you.
6. Explain that for *B* and *C*, the only possible answers are the 5 new words.

Word Building Pages 22, 28, 34, 42

1. Begin by discussing the Teaching Note in the margin of the pupil page.
2. Have the student look at the first word in *A*. Explain that we can form a new word by adding one or more letters. (On p. 22, *run* becomes *runs*.) Complete the exercise together.
3. Read the sentences in *B* aloud, and have the student read after you. Discuss the photo and have the student underline the sentence that describes the photo. Discuss why

sentences 2, 3, and 4 are not correct.
4. Explain that Unit 3 words *a* and *the* are used here because that's how people speak.
5. Point out that on this page the student is reading complete sentences. Explain that a sentence tells a complete idea, and begins with a capital letter and ends with a period.
6. Write a word from *A* on the board. Have the student circle the root word. Repeat with the other words from *A*.

Review Pages 23, 29, 35, 43

1. Write the sight words for review on the board. Pronounce them as the student follows along silently. Then read aloud together.
2. Point to each word on your list, and ask the student to tell you other words that start with the same letter.

3. Read the directions aloud and have the student read after you.
4. Have the student discuss each photo. The context of the photo will help to find the correct answer.

Unit 3

Sight Word Pages 45–49, 59–63

1. Read the new words aloud. Listen to the student repeat the words. Read the directions aloud and have the student read after you.
2. Discuss each photo in *A*. Have the student describe each photo. Read each group of phrases or sentences aloud, and have the student read after you. Point out that the words in **dark type** are the new words for that page. Ask the student to reread the sentences. On pp. 59–63, ask the student to write each new word after reading the sentence(s) smoothly.

3. In *B*, read each group of sentences aloud and have the student read after you. (In these sentences the new words are not in dark type.) Ask the student to decide which of the new words appears in each sentence by comparing the sentence to the list of new words at the top of the page. Tell the student to write (pp. 45–49) or underline (pp. 59–63) each new word after reading the sentence(s) smoothly. If a new word appears twice in one sentence, the student only writes it once.

Review Pages 50, 51, 57, 58, 64, 65, 71, 72

1. Write the sight words from the previous pages on the board. Read the words and have the student read after you. Go over the list until the student can read it unassisted.
2. On pp. 50, 57, 64, and 71, have the student discuss each photo. Read the incomplete sentence(s) below each photo aloud to the student and ask the student to reread it. Tell the student that one of the two words below the writing line correctly completes each sentence. Remind the student to use the context of the photo and the rest of the sentence to find the correct answer. Hint: say the sentence to yourself with each possible answer, and decide which word makes more sense.

As the unit progresses, the student will choose between groups of 2 words to complete a sentence (i.e., p. 57).
3. For pp. 51, 58, 65, and 72, explain that each group of sentences in *A* can be completed with a word from the box to the right. Have the student read the words in the box before reading the sentences. Discuss that there is no photo to help figure out the answer, but the rest of the sentence gives clues to the correct answer. Some word boxes have more choices than are needed.

Read the paragraph in *B* to the student. Have the student read after you. Ask simple recall questions to make sure the student understands the sentences.

Practice Pages 52–56, 66–70

1. Remind the student that this page gives further practice with words the student has studied before.
2. Read the words aloud. Listen to the student repeat the words.
3. In *A*, read each numbered group of sentences to the student, and have the student reread them. Emphasize that each group of sentences tells a story. Read through the exercise once, then return to the first group of sentences with writing lines to the right. Ask the student to decide which practice word appears in each sentence by comparing the sentence to the words at the top of the page. If a practice word appears twice in one sentence,

the student only writes it once. Remind the student to use a capital letter when the practice word is capitalized in the sentence. Have the student read the sentences in *A* again.
4. In *B*, read each group of sentences aloud, and have the student read after you. Study the photo together and discuss which group of sentences best describes it. Assist the student in writing the correct sentences. Then have the student reread the sentences. Discuss why the other choices are incorrect.
5. On pp. 67, 68, and 69, point out which practice words start with the same consonant sound.

Placement and Evaluation

Deciding which book is appropriate for a student entering a new reading program is never easy. To build success and confidence, place the adult in the book you are sure he or she can read with ease at the independent reading level. Follow these suggestions for initial placement.

Placing Your Student

1. Use all information available about your student such as standardized test scores on the Test of Adult Basic Education, the Adult Basic Learning Examination, the Wide Range Achievement Test, the Stanford Diagnostic Reading Test, or the California Adult Student Assessment System.
2. You may wish to administer an informal reading inventory such as the Slosson Oral Reading Test on an individualized basis. Match the student's reading level to our *Reading for Today* books.
3. You can ask your student to read the alphabet and a list of the key words for alphabet letters in *Book 1*. Any student experiencing difficulty should begin with *Book 1*.
4. You can administer individually the Diagnostic Placement Form located on the inside back cover of this *Teacher's Edition*. Make two photocopies, one for you to mark on and one for the student to read. Ask the student to read the *Book 1* word list. If the student knows these words, proceed to the next list. If a student misses three consecutive words, stop. Place the student in that book.
5. You may also wish to photocopy and administer the final reviews at the back of each student book. The final reviews contain words from each word recognition skill page.

Evaluating Your Student

1. You can informally check the student's progress by reviewing the adult's completed work after he or she has checked the correct answers. Listen to your student read the unit's culminating story, which requires applying all the skills covered in that unit.
2. Administer the final review at the end of each unit for a more formal evaluation. As a later check on whether the student has retained these skills to the end of the book, you may wish to initially photocopy the final reviews to administer twice—once at the end of the unit and again at the end of the book.
3. Students who need further practice for skill mastery can use the companion series *Communication for Today*, as well as additional practice books.

Reading for Today

A Sequential **1** Program for Adults

TEACHER'S EDITION

Program Authors	Jim Beers
	Linda Beech
	Tara McCarthy
	Sam V. Dauzat
	Jo Ann Dauzat
Teacher's Edition Author	Norman Najimy
Program Consultant	Donna Amstutz
Program Advisors	Lonnie Farrell
	Aryola Taylor
	Adriana Figueroa
	Carol Paggi
	Jean Batey
	Ann Reed
	Sharon Darling
	Susan Paull

STECK-VAUGHN COMPANY
AUSTIN, TEXAS
A Division of National Education Corporation

Acknowledgements

Cover Photography—Jim Myers

Contributing Photographers
George Berry
Jerry Jones
Phyllis Liedeker
Beverly Logan
Rick Williams
Sandy Wilson
Kurt Johnson

Illustration
Scott Bieser

Alphabet

Aa	Bb	Cc	Dd	Ee
Ff	Gg	Hh	Ii	Jj
Kk	Ll	Mm	Nn	Oo
Pp	Qq	Rr	Ss	Tt
Uu	Vv	Ww	Xx	Yy
		Zz		

ISBN 0-8114-1901-0

Table of Contents

UNIT 1
Letters

the alphabet, which appears on p. 2.

GETTING STARTED

This unit introduces students to consonant letters and beginning consonant sounds. Before proceeding, make sure students are familiar with the alphabet, which appears on p. 2. Throughout this unit, emphasize the beginning sound as you read each word. Emphasize the association between the letter and the beginning sound. When students can see a consonant letter and immediately say the sound, they have reached mastery of this unit's goals.

Make sure students understand that each letter can be written two different ways (capital letter and small letter). Both forms of the letter stand for the same sound.

See "Teaching Notes" in the front of this book for specific directions for teaching this unit.

Letters: B b, C c

STUDENT OBJECTIVE

Master the sounds for the consonants *b* and *c*, using the key words *bed* and *car*

B b bed

Look at this photo. Name the things that begin with the b sound.

Write the letter for the beginning sound.

b̲ed

Answers: bus, boy, bicycle, bag

C c car

Look at this photo. Name the things that begin with the c sound.

Write the letter for the beginning sound.

c̲ar

Answers: calendar, calculator, comb, camera

Letters: D d, F f

Master the sounds for the consonants *d* and *f*, using the key words *dog* and *food*

Phonics: Have students call out people's or place names that begin with *d* or *f*. If students have difficulty, make up the list yourself. Start by using students' names if possible. Write them on the board. (Explain that names of people and places begin with a capital letter.) Read the list aloud and have students repeat after you in chorus. Go over the list several times.

D d dog

Look at this photo. Name the things that begin with the d sound.

Write the letter for the beginning sound.

<u>d</u>og

Answers: dog, dish, desk, door

F f food

Look at this photo. Name the things that begin with the f sound.

Write the letter for the beginning sound.

<u>f</u>ood

Answers: fan, fish, fork, feathers

Letters: G g, H h

Master the sounds for the consonants *g* and *h*, using the key words *go* and *home*

1. Phonics: Have students look in magazines and newspapers for words beginning with *g* or *h*. Students do not have to read the word, only recognize the beginning letter. Write the words on the board. Read the list aloud and have students read after you in chorus.

2. If they need the practice, have students write each letter (*G*, *g*, *H*, *h*) several times in their notebooks.

G g　go

Look at this photo. Name the things that begin with the g sound.

Write the letter for the beginning sound.

<u>g</u>o

Answers: garage, guitar, gas can, garbage can

H h　home

Answers: hat, headband, hamburger, hot dog

Look at this photo. Name the things that begin with the h sound.

Write the letter for the beginning sound.

<u>h</u>ome

Letters: J j, K k

STUDENT OBJECTIVE

Master the sounds for the consonants *j* and *k*, using the key words *job* and *key*

ACTIVITIES

1. Phonics: Obtain several large index cards (4″ x 6″). Write the consonants *j* and *k* on one side of each card (make more than one card for each consonant). On the other side, write the key word or a word associated with the photo. Show the letter side and have students say the name of the letter. Show the other side, tell students the word, and have them repeat it after you.

2. Remind students to look for actions (kiss) as well as objects in the *k* photo.

J j   job

Look at this photo. Name the things that begin with the j sound.

Write the letter for the beginning sound.

<u>j</u>ob

Answers: jeans, jeep, jack, jacket

K k   key

Look at this photo. Name the things that begin with the k sound.

Write the letter for the beginning sound.

<u>k</u>ey

Answers: kitchen, kettle, key, kiss

Letters: L l, M m

STUDENT OBJECTIVE

Master the sounds for the consonants *l* and *m*, using the key words *light* and *money*

ACTIVITIES

1. Phonics: Ask students to think of names of people or places that begin with *l* or *m*. If students have difficulty, make up the list yourself. Start by using students' names if possible. Read the list aloud and have students repeat after you. Go over the list several times.

2. In the *l* photo, one of the words describes the whole scene. Guide students to use clues in the photo to determine that the scene is a library.

L l  light

Look at this photo. Name the things that begin with the l sound.

Write the letter for the beginning sound.

<u>l</u>ight

Answers: library, lamp, letter, list

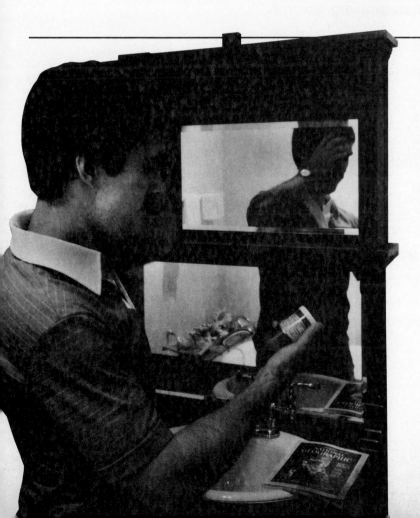

M m money

Look at this photo. Name the things that begin with the m sound.

Write the letter for the beginning sound.

<u>m</u>oney

Answers: man, medicine, mirror, magazine

Review: pages 5–9

A. Read the words below. Then look at the photo. Draw a line to match each word with the object it names.

car
dog
food
key
light

B. Say the name of each object shown below. Then write the letter for the beginning sound.

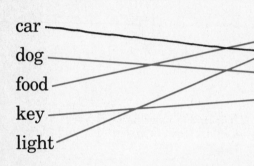         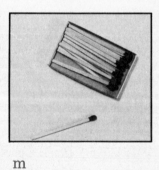

c   f   d   m

C. Draw a line to match the words that are the same.

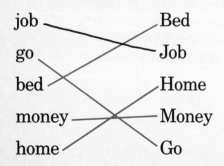

job   Bed
go   Job
bed   Home
money   Money
home   Go

D. Read the word in the first column. Then write the first letter.

light   _l_ight
bed   _b_ed
food   _f_ood
dog   _d_og
home   _h_ome

Letters: N n, P p

Master the sounds for the consonants *n* and *p*, using the key words *nurse* and *people*

1. Phonics: Ask students to think of objects in their room or apartment whose names start with *n* or *p*. Write the words on the board. Read the list aloud and have students read after you in chorus.

2. If they need the practice, have students write each letter (*N, n, P, p*) several times in their notebooks.

N n nurse

Look at this photo. Name the things that begin with the n sound.

Write the letter for the beginning sound.

<u>n</u>urse

Answers: notepad, nine, nickels, newspaper, nuts

P p  people

Look at this photo. Name the things that begin with the p sound.

Write the letter for the beginning sound.

<u>p</u>eople

Answers: person (or people), pizza, purse, picture, pen

12

Letters: Qu qu, R r

Master the sounds for the consonants *qu* and *r*, using the key words *quarter* and *radio*

Phonics: Have students take a mental trip to the supermarket and tell what they might buy whose names start with *r*. (Explain that very few words start with *qu*.) Write the words on the board (raisins, root beer, roast beef, radishes). Read the list aloud and have students read after you in chorus.

Qu qu quarter

Look at this photo. Name the things that begin with the qu sound.

Write the letter for the beginning sound.

<u>q</u> <u>u</u>arter

Answers: quart of milk,
quarters of pie,
quarters, quilt

R r radio

Look at this photo. Name the things that begin with the r sound.

Write the letter for the beginning sound.

<u>r</u>adio

Answers: running, road, radio,
roof

Letters: S s, T t

Master the sounds for the consonants *s* and *t*, using the key words *sick* and *table*

1. Phonics: Ask students to imagine they are walking down the street, and tell you things they might see whose names begin with *s* or *t* (signs, sidewalks, sun, shoes, streets, stores, tires, traffic, T-shirts, trees, trucks).

Write the words on the board. Read the list aloud and have students read after you in chorus.

2. If they need the practice, have students write each letter (*S, s, T, t*) several times in their notebooks.

S s  sick

Look at this photo. Name the things that begin with the s sound.

Write the letter for the beginning sound.

<u>s</u>ick

Answers: sandwich, soup, salad, salt

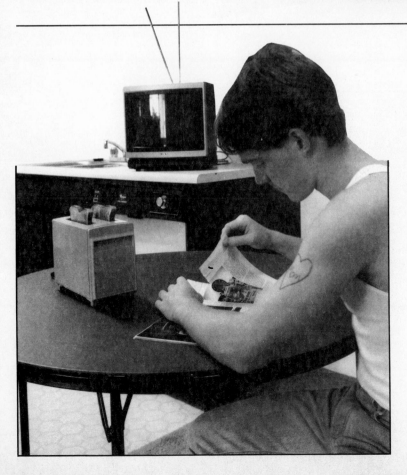

T t  table

Look at this photo. Name the things that begin with the t sound.

Write the letter for the beginning sound.

<u>t</u>able

Answers: table, tattoo, toaster, toast, television

Letters: V v, W w

STUDENT OBJECTIVE	ACTIVITIES

Master the sounds for the consonants *v* and *w*, using the key words *van* and *water*

1. Phonics: Have students look in magazines and newspapers for words beginning with *v* and *w*. Students do not have to read the words, only recognize the beginning letter. Write the words on the board. Read the list aloud and have students read aloud after you in chorus.

2. Introduce the letter *x*. Tell students that *x* is found at the end of words, such as *box*, *ax*, and *six*.

V v van

Look at this photo. Name the things that begin with the v sound.

Write the letter for the beginning sound.

<u>v</u>an

Answers: vest, van, valentine, vase

W w  water

Look at this photo. Name the things that begin with the w sound.

Write the letter for the beginning sound.

<u>w</u>ater

Answers: woman, window, watch, wall, wagon

Letters: Y y, Z z

STUDENT OBJECTIVE
Master the sounds for the consonants *y* and *z*, using the key words *yell* and *zipper*

ACTIVITY
Phonics: Explain that not many common words start with *y* or *z*. Ask students to think of objects or places whose names begin with *y* and *z* (zip code, zigzag, zinc, yawn, yolk, yes). If students have difficulty, tell them the words. Write the words on the board. Read the list aloud and have students read aloud after you in chorus.

Y y   yell

Look at this photo. Name the things that begin with the y sound.

Write the letter for the beginning sound.

y_ell

Answers: yarn, yardstick, yo-yo

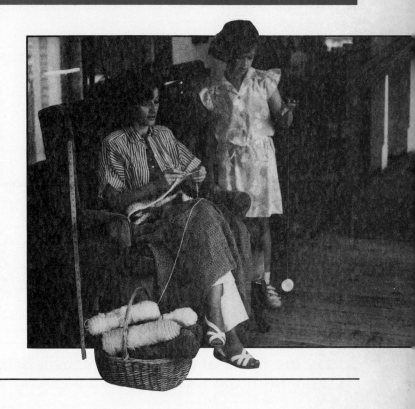

Z z   zipper

Look at this photo. Name the things that begin with the z sound.

Write the letter for the beginning sound.

z_ipper

Answers: zebra, zoo, zero, zipping

Review: pages 11–15

STUDENT OBJECTIVES

Review consonant sounds n–z; apply consonant sounds to new words; review key words and capital letters

ACTIVITY

Discuss simple rules of capitalization.

REINFORCEMENT & PRACTICE

After students complete this unit, assign Unit 1 in the accompanying workbook, *Communication for Today*. The workbook provides additional reading and writing activities.

A. Read the words below. Then look at the photo. Draw a line to match each word with the object it names.

nurse

sick

table

water

radio

quarter

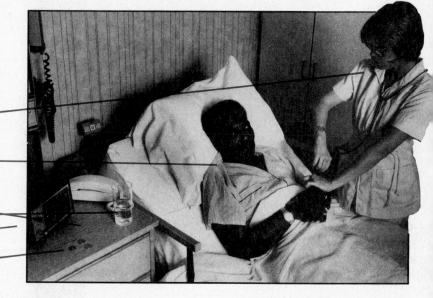

B. Say the name of each object shown below. Then write the letter for the beginning sound.

r   w   p   t

C. Draw a line to match the words that are the same.

people   Zipper

zipper   Van

yell   People

van   Quarter

quarter   Yell

D. Read the words in the first column. Then write the first letter.

table   <u>t</u>able

radio   <u>r</u>adio

zipper   <u>z</u>ipper

sick   <u>s</u>ick

van   <u>v</u>an

GETTING STARTED

1. In Unit 1, students learned consonant sounds at the beginning of words. In Unit 2, students memorize a bank of sight words. Words in this unit should be memorized *as whole words* in connection with the photos and activities. They should *not* be sounded out. As you proceed, continue to have students listen for beginning consonant sounds. In *Book 2*, students will combine their knowledge of consonant sounds and their sight word bank to begin the phonics strand of this program.

2. Since objects in the photo and activities within exercises are numbered, make sure students can recognize and say the numbers 1–5.
3. Each lesson in Unit 2 is 2 pages, and teaches 5 sight words. Some words are new, and some were introduced in Unit 1.

The large photo on each left-hand page illustrates the 5 new words. Students will have the oral language to *name* the things in the photo. When they have done so, ask them to *read* the words for the things they have just named. This will help them to see the relationship between the spoken and written word.

Remind students to look for action words (*run*), descriptive words (*big*), and words that describe the whole scene (*job*) in these photos.

See "Teaching Notes" in the front of this book for specific directions for teaching this unit.

Sight Words:

ACTIVITIES

Phonics: a. Point out that in *stand* the letters *s* and *t* go together to stand for the beginning sound they hear. (Other examples: *stop, store.*)

| big | man | run | sit | stand |

A. Look at the photo.
Look at the words.
Say each word.
Listen for the beginning sound.

B. Look at the words in the photo.
Below, write each word next to the correct number.
Then say each word.

1. r u n
2. m a n
3. b i g
4. s t a n d
5. s i t

b. Give students 5 index cards with one new word written on each. To see if students can recognize the beginning consonant sounds, say 3 similar words (*sun*, *run*, *fun*). Ask students to hold up the card for *run* when they hear the word. To test word recognition, say three dissimi- lar words (*run*, *dog*, *bed*). Again, have students hold up the card for *run* when they hear the word. Repeat with *man* and *sit*.

A. Read the new words on page 18.
Use the photo to help you.

B. Write the first letter of each new word.
Then write the word.

1. b ig   r un   s it
   b i g   r u n   s i t

   m an   s tand
   m a n   s t a n d

C. Write the new word that goes with each photo.

2. _____ sit _____

3. _____ stand _____

1. _____ man _____

4. _____ run _____

5. _____ big _____

Sight Words:

STUDENT OBJECTIVES

Master 2 new sight words: *can*, *stop*; review 3 Unit 1 words: *go*, *food*, *table*

ACTIVITIES

1. Phonics: Ask students to name other words that start with *c*, *g*, *f*, and *t*. Write them on the board. Read the list and have students read after you.

can	go	stop	food	table

A. Look at the photo.
Look at the words.
Say each word.
Listen for the beginning sound.

4. food

3. table

5. can

1. stop

2. go

B. Look at the words in the photo.
Below, write each word next to the correct number.
Then say each word.

1. <u>s t o p</u>

2. <u>g o</u>

3. <u>t a b l e</u>

4. <u>f o o d</u>

5. <u>c a n</u>

Point out that *stop* has the same beginning sound as *stand*.
2. Have students write each new word on an index card, and practice reading the words with each other, or at home.
3. Dictation: Tell students they will now practice writing the new words as they listen to you say them. Ask them to close their books for this activity.

Say the word *can*. Pause. Say the word again in a short sentence. Repeat the word. Ask students to write the word, spelling it as well as they can. Repeat with the rest of the words on the page. When students have finished, write the words on the board and have them correct their own work.

A. Read the new words on page 20.
Use the photo to help you.

B. Write the missing letters for each new word.
Then write the word.

1. f <u>o o d</u>
   <u>food</u>

2. t <u>a b l e</u>
   <u>t a b l e</u>

3. g <u>o</u>
   <u>g o</u>

4. c <u>a n</u>
   <u>c a n</u>

5. s <u>t o p</u>
   <u>s t o p</u>

C. Write the new word that goes with each photo.

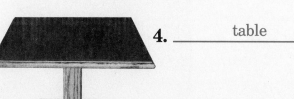

2. _____ can _____

3. _____ food _____

4. _____ table _____

1. _____ go _____

5. _____ stop _____

Word Building: Adding *s* to Action Words

STUDENT OBJECTIVE

Add inflectional ending *s* to regular verbs

TEACHING NOTE

Write the words *I run* and *You run* on the board. Read them aloud, and have students repeat after you. Then write the words *She run* and *He run*, read them aloud, and get students to respond that this "sounds funny" or "is not right." Rewrite the last two sentences to read *She runs* and *He runs*.

Ask what letter was added to *run* after *he* or *she* in the following: I *run*, you *run*, he *runs*, she *runs*.

**A. Add *s* to each word.
Then write the new word.**

1. run + **s** = run <u>S</u>   <u>runs</u>
2. sit + **s** = sit <u>s</u>   <u>sits</u>
3. stand + **s** = stand <u>s</u>   <u>stands</u>
4. stop + **s** = stop <u>s</u>   <u>stops</u>

**B. Read these words.
Then underline the words that
go with the photo.**

1. <u>A man runs.</u>
2. A man stops.
3. A man stands.
4. A man sits.

Review: pages 18–22

STUDENT OBJECTIVES

Review 10 new sight words; practice adding *s* to regular verbs

ACTIVITY

Ask students to make up their own sentences (or make them up yourself) using the words being reviewed.

For example: The people run. The dog sits. The man stands. Write the sentences on the board. Read them to the students, and have them read after you in chorus.

**A. Look at each photo.
Then read the words.
Write the word that
goes with each photo.**

1. ___stand___
stand   can

2. ___sit___
go   sit

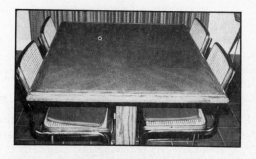

3. ___table___
food   table

4. ___run___
run   stop

**B. Look at each photo.
Then read the words.
Underline the words that go with the photo.
Then write the words.**

<u>A man sits.</u>
A man stands.

1. A man sits.

A man runs.
<u>A man stops.</u>

2. A man stops.

a big dog
<u>a big man</u>

3. a big man

Sight Words:

STUDENT OBJECTIVES
Master 3 new sight words: *use*, *walk*, *woman*; review 2 Unit 1 words: *home*, *key*

ACTIVITIES
1. Phonics: Ask: Which words on this page have the same beginning sound? What other words begin with *w*? If students hesitate, tell them some *w*

home	use	key	walk	woman

A. Look at the photo.
Look at the words.
Say each word.
Listen for the beginning sound.

1. woman
2. key
3. home
4. walk
5. use

B. Look at the words in the photo.
Below, write each word next to the correct number.
Then say each word.

1. w o m a n

2. k e y

3. h o m e

4. w a l k

5. u s e

words. Write the words on the board. Read the words aloud and have the students read after you in chorus.
2. Discussion: Ask simple questions about the photo on p. 24 that will get students to use the new words. For example: Who are these people? (an older woman and a younger woman) Where are they going? (home) How is she opening the door? (She is using the key.)
3. Have students write each new word on an index card, and practice reading the words with each other, or at home.

A. Read the new words on page 24.
   Use the photo to help you.

B. Write the first letter of each new word.
   Then write the word.

1. <u>h</u> ome
   <u>h o m e</u>

2. <u>w</u> alk
   <u>w a l k</u>

3. <u>u</u> se
   <u>u s e</u>

4. <u>k</u> ey
   <u>k e y</u>

5. <u>w</u> oman
   <u>w o m a n</u>

C. Write the new word that goes with each photo.

1. _____ key

2. _____ woman

4. _____ home

3. _____ walk

5. _____ use

Sight Words:

buy	dog	money	radio	yell

A. Look at the photo.
Look at the words.
Say each word.
Listen for the beginning sound.

B. Look at the words in the photo.
Below, write each word next to the correct number.
Then say each word.

1. r a d i o
2. d o g
3. y e l l
4. m o n e y
5. b u y

2. Discussion: Ask questions about the photo on p. 26. As students describe the photo, write the new sight words on the board. Read the words back to students, and ask them to point to each word at the top of the page as you read.
3. Dictation: Repeat the dictation activity outlined on p. 21, using the new words on p. 26.

A. Read the new words on page 26. Use the photo to help you.

B. Write the missing letters for each new word. Then write the word.

1. y <u>e l l</u>

　　<u>y e l l</u>

2. d <u>o g</u>

　　<u>d o g</u>

3. r <u>a d i o</u>

　　<u>r a d i o</u>

4. b <u>u y</u>

　　<u>b u y</u>

5. m <u>o n e y</u>

　　<u>m o n e y</u>

C. Write the new word that goes with each photo.

1. _____ dog _____

2. _____ money _____

3. _____ radio _____

4. _____ buy _____

5. _____ yell _____

Word Building: Adding *s* to Naming Words

STUDENT OBJECTIVES	TEACHING NOTE	
Add inflectional ending *s* to nouns; understand concept of plural nouns	Show the students one key, and write the word *key* on the board. Then show them two or more keys.	Get students to respond that we say *keys* when we have more than one, and write *keys* on the board.

A. Add *s* to each word.
Then write the new word.

1. home + **s** = home_s_   homes

2. key   + **s** = key_s_   keys

3. dog   + **s** = dog_s_   dogs

4. table + **s** = table_s_   tables

5. radio + **s** = radio_s_   radios

B. Read these words.
Then underline the words that go with the photo.

1. A man uses keys.

2. The man buys radios.

3. The woman buys tables.

4. A woman stops the dogs.

5. The dogs run.

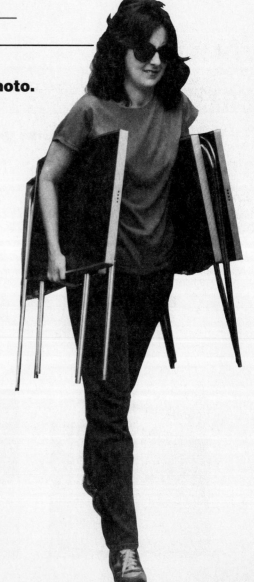

Review: pages 24–28

STUDENT OBJECTIVES

Review 10 new sight words; practice adding *s* to nouns

ACTIVITIES

Write each word of a sentence from this page onto an index card. Scramble the sentence and have students unscramble it. Repeat with several of the sentences from this page.

A. Look at each photo.
Then read the words.
Write the word that goes with each photo.

1. The man uses ___money___ .

key money

2. A ___woman___ walks home.

woman radio

3. The woman ___yells___ .

buys yells

4. The man ___uses___ a radio.

uses yells

B. Look at each photo.
Then read the words.
Underline the words that go with the photo.
Then write the words.

A man buys dogs.
A man buys radios.

The dogs sit.
The dogs walk.

A woman uses keys.
A woman uses money.

1. ___A man buys radios.___   **2.** ___The dogs sit.___   **3.** ___A woman uses keys.___

30

Sight Words:

STUDENT OBJECTIVE
Master 5 new sight words

ACTIVITIES
1. Phonics: Ask students which two words on these pages have the same beginning sound. Ask them to name other words that start with c. Write the words the

brother   car   country   sister   work

A. Look at the photo.
Look at the words.
Say each word.
Listen for the beginning sound.

B. Look at the words in the photo.
Below, write each word next to the correct number.
Then say each word.

1. b r o t h e r
2. c o u n t r y
3. w o r k
4. c a r
5. s i s t e r

students say on the board. Read them aloud and have them read after you in chorus.
2. Discussion: Explain that *country* has more than one meaning. (A specific nation: Mexico, the United States; a non-city area with trees, grass, space, less traffic, no tall buildings, fewer people)
3. Dictation: Repeat the dictation activity outlined on p. 21, using the new words on p. 30.

A. Read the new words on page 30. Use the photo to help you.

B. Write the missing letters for each new word. Then write the word.

1. c a r
   c a r

2. s i s t e r
   s i s t e r

3. w o r k
   w o r k

4. b r o t h e r
   b r o t h e r

5. c o u n t r y
   c o u n t r y

C. Write the new word that goes with each photo.

1. _____brother_____

3. _____country_____

2. _____sister_____

4. _____car_____

5. _____work_____

Sight Words:

STUDENT OBJECTIVES

Master 3 new sight words: *family, help, look*; review 2 Unit 1 words: *van, water*

ACTIVITIES

1. Phonics: Give students 5 index cards with the new words written on them. To see if students can recognize the beginning consonant sounds, say

family	help	look	van	water

A. Look at the photo.
Look at the words.
Say each word.
Listen for the beginning sound.

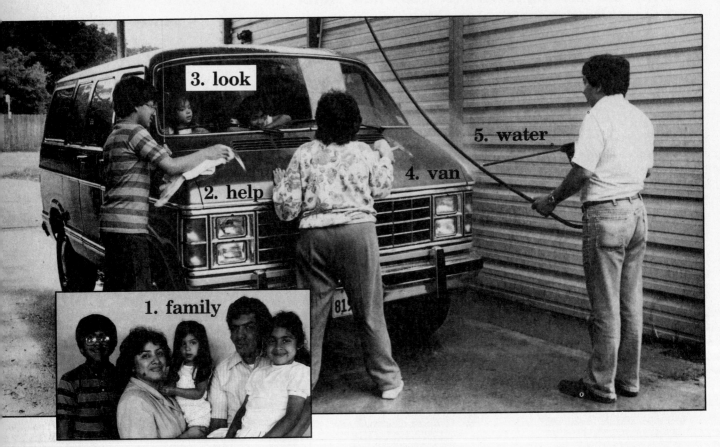

3. look
5. water
4. van
2. help
1. family

B. Look at the words in the photo.
Below, write each word next to the correct number.
Then say each word.

1. f a m i l y
2. h e l p
3. l o o k
4. v a n
5. w a t e r

three similar words (*look, took, book*). Students should hold up the card for *look* when they hear the word. To test word recognition, say three dissimilar words (*man, look, sit*). Again, have students hold up the card for *look* when they hear the word. Repeat with *van*.

2. Discussion: Ask simple questions about the photo on p. 32. For example: The van is dirty; could there be a special reason that the family is cleaning it? Why are the little children inside the van? What is each person doing? Encourage students to share experiences they have had that are similar to the one in the photo.

A. Read the new words on page 32. Use the photo to help you.

B. Write the first letter of each new word. Then write the word.

1. <u>v</u> an

<u>v</u> <u>a</u> <u>n</u>

2. <u>l</u> ook

<u>l</u> <u>o</u> <u>o</u> <u>k</u>

3. <u>w</u> ater

<u>w</u> <u>a</u> <u>t</u> <u>e</u> <u>r</u>

4. <u>h</u> elp

<u>h</u> <u>e</u> <u>l</u> <u>p</u>

5. <u>f</u> amily

<u>f</u> <u>a</u> <u>m</u> <u>i</u> <u>l</u> <u>y</u>

C. Write the new word that goes with each photo.

1. _____ look

3. _____ van

4. _____ family

2. _____ water

5. _____ help

Word Building: Adding *ed* to Words

STUDENT OBJECTIVES	TEACHING NOTE
Add inflectional ending *ed* to regular verbs; recognize past tense	Write the phrase *I work* on the board. Tell students that this describes the present time, what is happening now.

Ask students what they would say to describe work that they did yesterday. Get them to say *I worked*, and write this on the board. Explain that the most common way to indicate that something happened in the past is to add *ed* to action words.

Discuss the meaning of past time, and why it is difficult to show the past in a photo. Ask what about the photo itself gives us a hint of the past. (The people in the background are working. The people in the foreground are taking a break, indicating that they worked in the recent past.)

A. Add *ed* to each word. Then write the new word.

1. work + **ed** = work __ed__   worked

2. help + **ed** = help __ed__   helped

3. look + **ed** = look __ed__   looked

4. yell + **ed** = yell __ed__   yelled

5. walk + **ed** = walk __ed__   walked

B. Read these words. Then underline the words that go with the photo.

1. <u>The people worked.</u>
2. A dog walked.
3. A man walked.
4. The sister yelled.
5. The woman helped.

Review: pages 30–34

STUDENT OBJECTIVES

Review 10 new sight words; practice adding *ed* to regular verbs

ACTIVITIES

Discussion: In *A*, point out that the word *run* has different meanings. Discuss what it means for a person, a van, and water to run.

In *B*, note that these three photos and accompanying sentences tell a brief story. Point out the use of *ed* words to indicate the story happened in the past. Discuss what might happen next, if there were a fourth photo.

A. Look at each photo. Then read the words. Write the word that goes with each photo.

1. The cars ___go___

           go   table

3. The ___van___ runs.

     van   family

2. a ___country___ home

   food   country

4. The ___water___ runs.

    water   country

B. Look at each photo. Then read the words. Underline the words that go with the photo. Then write the words.

<u>The sister worked.</u>
The car worked.

<u>The water helped.</u>
<u>The brother helped.</u>

<u>The family looked.</u>
The family yelled.

1. The sister worked.

2. The brother helped.

3. The family looked.

Sight Words:

STUDENT OBJECTIVES

Master 2 new sight words: *get, well*; review 3 Unit 1 words: *bed, sick, nurse*

ACTIVITIES

1. Phonics: Read the new words and have students repeat after you in chorus. Then give an initial consonant sound and ask students to identify

bed	get	nurse	well	sick

A. Look at the photo.
Look at the words.
Say each word.
Listen for the beginning sound.

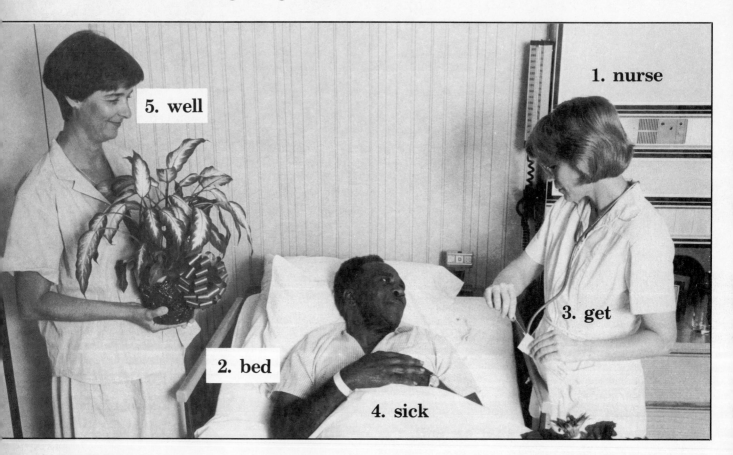

5. well

1. nurse

3. get

2. bed

4. sick

B. Look at the words in the photo.
Below, write each word next to the correct number.
Then say each word.

1. n u r s e
2. b e d
3. g e t
4. s i c k
5. w e l l

the word that begins with that sound.

2. Present a sentence about the photo on p. 36 and ask students to supply the new word that is missing. For example, The person in bed feels _____ .

3. Have students write each new word on an index card, and practice reading the words with each other, or at home.

A. Read the new words on page 36.
Use the photo to help you.

B. Write the missing letters for each new word.
Then write the word.

1. b <u>e</u> <u>d</u>
<u>b</u> <u>e</u> <u>d</u>

2. g <u>e</u> <u>t</u>
<u>g</u> <u>e</u> <u>t</u>

3. w <u>e</u> <u>l</u> <u>l</u>
<u>w</u> <u>e</u> <u>l</u> <u>l</u>

4. n <u>u</u> <u>r</u> <u>s</u> <u>e</u>
<u>n</u> <u>u</u> <u>r</u> <u>s</u> <u>e</u>

5. s <u>i</u> <u>c</u> <u>k</u>
<u>s</u> <u>i</u> <u>c</u> <u>k</u>

C. Write the new word that goes with each photo.

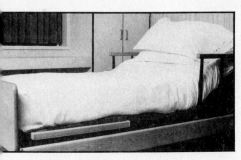

1. _____ bed _____

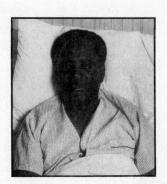

2. _____ well _____

3. _____ nurse _____

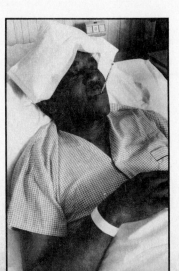

4. _____ sick _____

5. _____ get _____

Sight Words:

STUDENT OBJECTIVE	ACTIVITIES
Master 5 new sight words	**1. Phonics:** Point out that although *city* starts with *c*, it has a different beginning sound than *car*. When *e* or *i* follows *c*, the sound we hear is the /s/ sound. Other

bus   city   like   pay   store

A. Look at the photo.
    Look at the words.
    Say each word.
    Listen for the beginning sound.

B. Look at the words in the photo.
    Below, write each word next to the correct number.
    Then say each word.

1. p a y
2. l i k e
3. b u s
4. c i t y
5. s t o r e

examples: *circus, circle, cent, cement.*
2. Discussion: Explain the difference in meaning between *pay*, introduced here, and *buy*, introduced on p. 26. We *pay* someone for work they do, or for something they give us. When we *buy* something, we *pay* for it with money.

3. Dictation: Repeat the dictation activity outlined on p. 21, using the new words on p. 38.

A. Read the new words on page 38. Use the photo to help you.

B. Write the first letter of each new word. Then write the word.

1. <u>c</u> ity
<u>c</u> <u>i</u> <u>t</u> <u>y</u>

2. <u>l</u> ike
<u>l</u> <u>i</u> <u>k</u> <u>e</u>

3. <u>p</u> ay
<u>p</u> <u>a</u> <u>y</u>

4. <u>b</u> us
<u>b</u> <u>u</u> <u>s</u>

5. <u>s</u> tore
<u>s</u> <u>t</u> <u>o</u> <u>r</u> <u>e</u>

C. Write the new word that goes with each photo.

1. <u>   store   </u>

2. <u>   like   </u>

3. <u>   city   </u>

4. <u>   pay   </u>

5. <u>   bus   </u>

Sight Words:

STUDENT OBJECTIVES

Master 2 new sight words: *bills, boss*; review 3 Unit 1 words: *job, light, people*

ACTIVITIES

1. Phonics: Ask students which of these words have the same beginning sound. Have them tell you other words that start with *b*. Write the words on

bills   boss   job   light   people

A. Look at the photo.
Look at the words.
Say each word.
Listen for the beginning sound.

1. light

4. job

3. boss

5. bills

2. people

B. Look at the words in the photo.
Below, write each word next to the correct number.
Then say each word.

1. l i g h t
2. p e o p l e
3. b o s s
4. j o b
5. b i l l s

the board, then read the list together.
2. Ask students to make up their own sentences (or make them up yourself) using the new words. For example: The people work. Write the sentences on the board. Read them to the students and have them read after you in chorus.

A. Read the new words on page 40.
   Use the photo to help you.

B. Write the missing letters for each new word.
   Then write the word.

1. p <u>e o p l e</u>
   <u>p e o p l e</u>

2. b <u>i l l s</u>
   <u>b i l l s</u>

3. l <u>i g h t</u>
   <u>l i g h t</u>

4. b <u>o s s</u>
   <u>b o s s</u>

5. j <u>o b</u>
   <u>j o b</u>

C. Write the new word that goes with each photo.

1. <u>bills</u>

2. <u>people</u>

3. <u>light</u>

4. <u>boss</u>

5. <u>job</u>

Word Building: Adding *ing* to Words

STUDENT OBJECTIVES

Adding inflectional ending *ing* to regular verbs

TEACHING NOTE

Write the sentence *I walk* on the board. Explain that this sentence describes something that happens continually—every day. (I walk to work).

Then ask students to tell you what you are doing as you walk across the room (You are walking). Next, look out a window, or do other obvious things. Get students to give you verbs with *ing* endings.

Write the sentence *I am walking* on the board. Point out that after words like *am*, *is*, *are*, *was*, and *were*, we usually add *ing* to the word that follows. Explain that we usually use *ing* words to answer the question, "What are you doing?"

A. Add *ing* to each word. Then write the new word.

1. walk + ing = walk _ing_ walking
2. pay + ing = pay _ing_ paying
3. look + ing = look _ing_ looking
4. help + ing = help _ing_ helping
5. yell + ing = yell _ing_ yelling
6. work + ing = work _ing_ working

B. Read these words. Then underline the words that go with the photo.

1. a woman looking
2. the people yelling
3. the man paying
4. the dog walking
5. a sister working

Review: pages 36–42

STUDENT OBJECTIVES

Review 15 new sight words; practice adding *ing* to regular verbs

ACTIVITY

Write each word of a sentence from this page onto an index card. Scramble the sentence and have students unscramble it. Repeat with several of the sentences from this page.

REINFORCEMENT & PRACTICE

After students complete this unit, assign Unit 2 in the accompanying workbook, *Communication for Today.* The workbook provides additional reading and writing activities based on sight words in this unit.

**A. Look at each photo.
Then read the words.
Write the word that goes with each photo.**

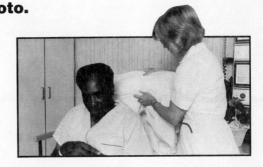

1. People ___pay___ bills.
   pay   like

2. A nurse helps a ___sick___ man.
   sick   store

3. The man ___gets___ a job.
   go   gets

4. The city ___bus___ runs well.
   bus   bed

**B. Look at each photo.
Then read the words.
Underline the words that go with the photo.
Then write the words.**

a man buying food
a man buying a car

the boss working
the boss paying

a woman walking
a bed walking

1. a man buying food
2. the boss paying
3. a woman walking

UNIT 3
Words and Sentences

GETTING STARTED

1. This unit continues the sight word approach of Unit 2, and is organized as follows: sight words, practice of sight words, then review.
2. Sight word pages introduce 3 or 4 new words. Students will now read

complete sentences on every page.

In Units 1 & 2, there is a direct connection between the new word and the photo. In Unit 3, the photo can only hint at the correct answer. Students must use the context of the sentence to determine the answer.
3. Practice pages present the words

from sight word pages in new combinations, giving students further opportunities to read and write these words in different contexts.
4. Review pages conclude each sight word and practice section.
5. Pages 73–76 introduce the number words one through ten.

6. Page 77 is a final review of *Book 1*, and emphasizes beginning consonant sounds.
7. Pages 78–79 contain a story using the words taught in *Book 1*.
8. See "Teaching Notes" in the front of this book for specific directions for teaching this unit.

Sight Words:

STUDENT OBJECTIVE
Master 3 new sight words

ACTIVITY
Phonics: Point out that in the word *the*, the letters *t* and *h* go together to stand for a new sound (not a blend of *t* and *h*), such as in *this, that, they*. Have students listen to the difference in beginning sounds between *this* and *take*.

a   an   the

A. Read the words.
Use the photos to help you.

1. a man
     the man

2. a car
     the car

3. a bus
     the bus

4. a woman
     the woman

5. a radio
     the radio

6. a key
     the key

B. Read the word.
Then say the name of the object shown.

1. an

2. an

3. an

Sight Words:

STUDENT OBJECTIVE
Master 3 new sight words

ACTIVITIES
1. Comprehension: In *A*, #3, ask: Why are the cars stopped? What would happen if they didn't stop?
2. Write sentences from this page on the board, using students' names. Have a volunteer rewrite using *he* and *she*.

and   he   she

A. Look at each photo. Then read the sentences.

1. **He** runs.
   She runs.
   He and she run.

2. **She** works.
   He works.
   She and he work.

3. **He** stops the car.
   She stops the car.
   He and she stop.

4. **He** sits.
   She sits.
   He and she sit.

B. Read these sentences. Write the new words.

1. She sits. ___She___

   He stands. ___He___

   She sits, and he stands. ___She___ ___and___ ___he___

2. He likes the car. ___He___

   She likes the van. ___She___

   He likes the car, and she likes the van. ___He___ ___and___ ___she___

3. He gets the food. ___He___

   She gets the water. ___She___

   He gets the food, and she gets the water. ___He___ ___and___ ___she___

Sight Words:

ACTIVITIES
1. Discussion: Explain that *is* and *are* indicate that something is happening now. *Was* indicates something that happened in the past.
2. Write each word of a sentence from this page on index cards. Scramble the sentence and have students unscramble it. Repeat with several sentences from the page.

is   was   are

A. Look at each photo. Then read the sentences.

1. The man **is** sick.
   The man and woman **are** sick.

2. The man **is** walking.
   The dog **was** walking.

3. The woman **is** standing.
   The man **was** standing.

4. The man **is** home.
   The man and woman **are** home.

B. Read these sentences. Write the new words.

1. The man is walking. _____is_____

   The woman was walking. _____was_____

   The man and the dog are walking. _____are_____

2. The man was sick. _____was_____

   The woman is sick. _____is_____

   The nurse and the man are well. _____are_____

3. The brother and sister are yelling. _____are_____

   The man was yelling. _____was_____

   The woman is yelling. _____is_____

Sight Words:

I   you   they

**A. Look at each photo.
Then read the sentences.**

1. **You** and **I** buy food.

2. **I** sit, and **you** stand.

3. **I** look, and **they** run.

4. **They** help the man.

**B. Read these sentences.
Write the new words.**

1. You and I can get a job. _____You_____ _____I_____

2. I can use the bus. _____I_____

3. They can go home. _____They_____

4. You and I like the car. _____You_____ _____I_____

5. They can pay bills. _____They_____

Sight Words:

ACTIVITIES
1. Make up sentences using *this* and *that* to describe objects in the room. After each sentence, ask students which object is closer and which is farther away.
2. In *A*, #3 & 4, make sure students understand *it* refers to the dog and the van.

this   that   it

Make up groups of sentences using the word *it*. (This is her car. She likes *it*.) Ask students what *it* refers to in each grouping.

**A. Look at each photo.
Then read the sentences.**

1. **This** is a table, and **that** is a light.

2. **This** man works, and **that** man helps.

3. **This** is a dog.
   It likes food.

4. **This** is the van **that** I like.
   It runs well.

**B. Read these sentences.
Write the new words.**

1. This food bill is big. ____This____
   I can pay it. ____it____

2. This man works. ____This____
   That job pays money. ____That____

3. He likes this job, and she likes that job. ____this____ ____that____

4. She uses that car, and she likes it. ____that____ ____it____

5. Use this money, and buy that radio. ____this____ ____that____

Review: pages 45–49

STUDENT OBJECTIVE	ACTIVITY	answering sentence (there can be

STUDENT OBJECTIVE

Review 15 new sight words in sentences and photos

ACTIVITY

Ask questions that can be answered by reading a sentence from pp. 46–49. Ask volunteers to read the

answering sentence (there can be more than one). Do one page at a time. On p. 46 ask: Who likes the car? Who likes the van? On p. 47: Who feels well?

Look at each photo.
Then read the sentences.
Write the word that completes each sentence.

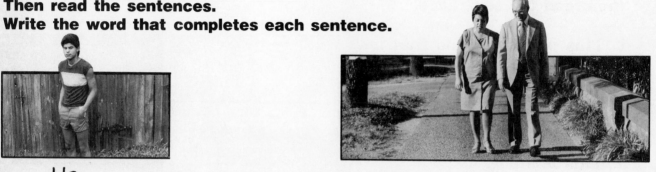

1. ___He___ is a man.

He   She

2. ___They___ walk.

They   This

3. She uses ___the___ key.

the   I

4. The man ___and___ woman
are standing.

a   and

5. That ___is___ a car.

it   is

6. I ___was___ standing.

was   you

7. ___I___ sit.

That   I

8. They ___are___ home.

are   am

Review: pages 45–49

STUDENT OBJECTIVE
Review 15 new sight words in sentences and a short paragraph

ACTIVITY
Discussion: Tell students that on this page they will read a paragraph. Explain that a paragraph is made up of sentences that give information about one idea. A paragraph is indented at the beginning. Show them a page from a book or newspaper with several paragraphs.

A. Look at the words in the word box.
Then read the sentences.
Write the word that completes each sentence.

1. The sister ___was___ home.

   ___A___ brother was working.

was	A
she	

2. ___He___ is a man.

   ___She___ is a woman.

   ___They___ are people.

She	They
Are	He

3. This is ___a___ zipper.

   ___It___ is big.

   ___I___ use it.

It	a
I	Was

4. ___Are___ you a nurse?

   ___Is___ she sick?

   ___You___ are well.

You	Is
Are	An

5. That is ___the___ money.

   I pay you the money, ___and___ you work.

   ___That___ work is a job.

That	and
the	I

B. Read this paragraph.
Underline the new words from the word box.

and	the
You	this

    I can use <u>this</u> van. He <u>and</u> she can use <u>the</u> car. <u>You</u> can use the bus. They are walking.

Practice:

you are   he is

**A. Read the sentences.
Write the new words.**

1. **You are** working.
   He is working.

   You are buying food.

   He is buying food.

You	are
He	is

2. **You are** paying a bill.
   He is paying a bill.
   He and **you are** paying bills.

   You are walking.

   He is walking.

   He and you are walking.

You	are
He	is
you	are

**B. Read these sentences.
Write the sentences that go with the photo.**

1. You are sick.
   He is well.
   They are well.

2. You are going home.
   He is going home.
   He and you are going home.

3. You are helping the man.
   He is helping the woman.
   You and he are helping people.

You are going home.

He is going home.

He and you are going home.

Practice:

STUDENT OBJECTIVE
Practice sight words in new contexts

ACTIVITY
Make up a simple sentence using students' names. Follow it with another sentence using *they*: John and Mary are walking. *They* like to walk. Get students to understand that the word *they* stands for John and Mary in the first sentence. Do another

they are   that is

group; this time ask a volunteer to fill in the blank: John and Mary go to the store. _____ buy food. Repeat with other examples.

**A. Read the sentences.
Write the new words.**

1. **They are** yelling.
   That is the woman yelling.

   They are working.   <u>They</u>   <u>are</u>

   That is a working man.   <u>That</u>   <u>is</u>

2. **They are** paying the bill.
   That is the man paying the bill.
   That is the bill that I pay.

   They are helping.   <u>They</u>   <u>are</u>

   That is the man helping the dog.   <u>That</u>   <u>is</u>

   That is the woman I helped.   <u>That</u>   <u>is</u>

**B. Read these sentences.
Write the sentences that go with the photo.**

1. That is the woman I like.
   That is the man I helped.
   They are walking.

2. That is the van I like.
   That is the car I like.
   They are working well.

3. That is the money.
   That is the light bill.
   They are paying the light bill.

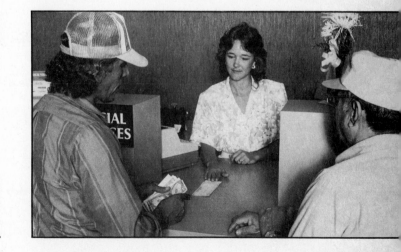

   <u>That is the money.</u>

   <u>That is the light bill.</u>

   <u>They are paying the light bill.</u>

Practice:

STUDENT OBJECTIVE
Practice sight words in new contexts

ACTIVITY
Discussion: Contrast *this is* with *that is* (p. 53). Point to an object near to you and say: This is a _____. Then point to something at the back of the room and say: That is a _____. Have students make up other sentences about objects in the room.

she and I   this is

A. Read the sentences.
Write the new words.

1. **This is** the bus.
   She and I use the bus.
   This is the bus **she and I** use.

   This is the boss.   This _____   is _____

   This is the store.   This _____   is _____

   She and I work.   She _____   and _____   I _____

2. **This is** a woman.
   She and I walk.
   She and I like walking.

   This is a car.   This _____   is _____

   This is the car key.   This _____   is _____

   She and I use the key.   She _____   and _____   I _____

B. Read these sentences.
Write the sentences that go with the photo.

1. This is the car that I like.
   She and I use the car.

2. She and I buy the food.
   This is the food the family likes.

3. This is the car key.
   She and I get the key.

   She and I buy the food.

   This is the food the family likes.

Practice:

it was   a   the

pencil. Have students make up sentences about other objects in the room.

A. Read the sentences.
Write the new words.

1. **A** man walks.
   The bus stops.

   The city was big.   <u>The</u>

   It was a big city.   <u>It</u>   <u>was</u>   <u>a</u>

2. **The** people work.
   A boss pays **the** people.

   The brother stands.   <u>The</u>

   The sister sits.   <u>The</u>

3. **The** light was working.
   It was a light that worked well.

   A dog walked.   <u>A</u>

   It was walking.   <u>It</u>   <u>was</u>

B. Read these sentences.
Write the sentences that go with the photo.

1. The table was big.
   It was the family table.

2. The light bill was big.
   A woman was paying it.

3. The man is standing.
   A bus is going.

   The man is standing.

   A bus is going.

Practice:

this was   that was

Discussion: Contrast *this was* and *that was*, which describe the past, to *this is* and *that is*, which describe the present. Discuss the difficulty of illustrating the past in a photograph, and ask what was going on just before the photo in *B* was taken, and what will happen next.

**A. Read the sentences.
Write the new words.**

1. **This was** the woman, and **that was** the man.

   This was the bill, and   _____This_____   _____was_____

   that was the money.   _____that_____   _____was_____

2. **That was** the sister, and **this was** the brother.

   This was the bus, and   _____This_____   _____was_____

   that was the car.   _____that_____   _____was_____

3. **That was** work, and **this was** home.

   This was the city, and   _____This_____   _____was_____

   that was the country.   _____that_____   _____was_____

**B. Read these sentences.
Write the sentences that go with the photo.**

1. That was a home.
   This was a home.

2. This was the man I helped.
   That was the woman helping the dog.

3. That was the bus that was working.
   This was the car that was going.

   That was a home.

   This was a home.

Review: pages 52–56

STUDENT OBJECTIVE

Review 15 practice words in sentences and photos

ACTIVITY

Ask students to pick one of the photos and work together to make up a story about it, using the sentences under the photo within their story. Have them say what might have happened before and after the scene in the photo. Write the story on the board. Read it to the students, and have them read after you in chorus.

Look at each photo.
Then read the sentences.
Write the word or words that complete each sentence.

1. ____This is____ a car.

   This is   You are

____It was____ going.

   The   It was

2. ____That is____ a van.

   That is   You are

____She and I____ like the van.

   A   She and I

3. This is ____a____ dog.

   it was   a

____He is____ walking

   That was   He is

the dog.

4. They buy ____the____ radio.

   the   that was

____They are____ paying

   They are   This was

the money.

58

Review: pages 52–56

STUDENT OBJECTIVE

Review 15 practice words in sentences and a short paragraph

ACTIVITIES

1. Comprehension: Have students discuss the situation of the people in the paragraph. How are they related? Why are they discussing the bills? Emphasize that there is no one right answer.

2. Dictation: Repeat the dictation activity outlined on p. 21, using the words on pp. 52–56.

A. Look at the words in the word box.
Then read the sentences.
Write the word or words that complete each sentence.

1. _____You are_____ walking the dog.

   _____This is_____ a big job.

> You are
> The
> This is

2. _____He is_____ a nurse.

   _____She and I_____ helped the nurse.

> She and I
> He is
> A

3. The man was paying _____a_____ bill.

   _____It was_____ a big bill.

> They are
> It was
> a

4. _____That is_____ a big van.

   _____They are_____ buying the van.

   It is _____the_____ van I liked.

> They are
> the
> That is
> She and I

5. _____He is_____ buying food.

   She and I are buying _____a_____ radio.

> This was
> a
> He is

B. Read this paragraph.
Underline the new words from the word box.

That is the light bill. She and I
are paying it. That is the food bill.
They are paying that bill. You can
help pay the bills.

> That is
> the
> She and I
> They are

Sight Words:

STUDENT OBJECTIVE
Master 4 new sight words

ACTIVITY
Ask students to change one word in each sentence of A. For example, *The bus stops for the light* can be changed to *The car stops for the light*.

with	us	for	has

A. Look at each photo.
Read each sentence.
Then write the new word or words.

1. The bus stops **for** the light.

   _____for_____

2. The man sits **with** the woman.

   _____with_____

3. The woman **has** water.

   _____has_____

4. He runs **with us**.

   ___with___ ___us___

B. Read these sentences.
Underline the new words.

1. The brother walks with us.
   He has a sister.
   The sister walks with us.
   She has a radio.

2. The man sits with us.
   He has a dog.
   The woman sits with us.
   She walks with us.

3. The dog has a home.
   He sits for us.
   He runs with us.
   He likes us.

4. This woman works with us.
   She works for money.
   The boss has money.
   The boss pays us for working.

Sight Words:

STUDENT OBJECTIVE
Master 4 new sight words

ACTIVITY
Write sentences from this page on the board, using students' names. Have them rewrite the sentences using the correct pronouns.

to   him   her   them

**A. Look at each photo.
Read each sentence.
Then write the new word.**

1. The dog sits with **him.**

him

2. He is standing with **her.**

her

3. The van stops for **them.**

them

4. He walks **to** work.

to

**B. Read these sentences.
Underline the new words.**

1. The man helps her.
The woman helps him.

2. He walks to work with her.
She walks to work with him.
They go to work with them.

3. This woman walks to work.
She likes her job.
The boss pays her well.
She likes her.
She likes working for her.

Sight Words:

STUDENT OBJECTIVE
Master 4 new sight words

ACTIVITY
Discussion: Point out that *buy* (p. 26) and *by* sound alike but are spelled differently and have different meanings (buy: to shop; by: next to, go past).

by	from	me	we

**A. Look at each photo.
Read each sentence.
Then write the new word or words.**

1. Stop the car for **me**.

<u>   me   </u>

2. You can sit **by me**.

<u> by </u>   <u> me </u>

3. I get the key **from** the table.

<u> from </u>

4. **We** can go to the store.

<u> We </u>

**B. Read these sentences.
Underline the new words.**

1. Get the money <u>from</u> <u>me</u>.
Walk home with <u>me</u>.
The home is <u>by</u> the store.
You can go to the store for <u>me</u>.

2. He works with <u>me</u>.
He and I get money <u>by</u> working.
<u>We</u> get the money <u>from</u> the boss.
<u>We</u> go to the store.

3. He can go home <u>from</u> work.
He can walk with <u>me</u> to the bus stop.
<u>We</u> stand <u>by</u> the bus stop.
The bus runs <u>by</u> us.

4. <u>We</u> walk <u>by</u> the store.
<u>We</u> get food <u>from</u> the store.
The food is for <u>me</u>.
<u>We</u> like the food store.

Sight Words:

am   not   at   have

**A. Look at each photo.
Read the sentences.
Then write the new words.**

1. I **am** looking **at** the dog.
You are **not** looking **at** the dog.

am _____ at _____ not _____

2. I **am** working.
You are **not** working.

am _____ not _____

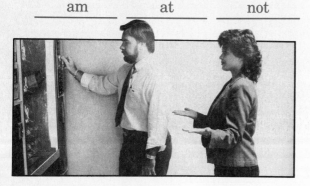

3. I can **not** buy it.
You **have** the quarter.

not _____ have _____

4. I **have** a car.
The car is **at** home.

have _____ at _____

**B. Read these sentences.
Underline the new words.**

1. I have a home.
I am going home.
I am not at work.

2. I have bills to pay.
I have money to pay them.
I am paying the bills.

3. I am going to work.
I am not walking to work.
I am standing at the bus stop.

4. I am at the store.
I am not buying a radio.
I have bills to pay.

Sight Words:

both   in   no   of

**A. Look at each photo.
Read each sentence.
Then write the new word or words.**

1. The man has **no** key.

_____no_____

2. The key is **in** the van.

_____in_____

3. Both of the sisters are walking.

____Both____ ____of____

4. Both of them use quarters.

____Both____ ____of____

**B. Read these sentences.
Underline the new words.**

1. We are in the store.
   Both of us have money.
   He has no money.

3. Both of us have cars.
   We use the cars in
   the country.
   Both of us use the bus in
   the city.

2. Both of us like the country.
   We have no work in
   the country.
   Both of us work in the city.

4. Both of us have quarters.
   Both of us use the quarters.
   We buy zippers at the store.

64

Review: pages 59–63

Review 20 new sight words in sentences and paragraphs

Ask questions that can be answered by reading a sentence from pp. 59–63. Ask volunteers to read the answering sentence (there can be more than one). Do one page at a time. On p. 59 ask: Who has a radio? On p. 60: Where is the man walking to?

Look at each photo.
Then read the sentences.
Write the word that completes each sentence.

1. The brothers work ___at___ the
at   from

store. They work ___with___ us.
them   with

2. Both ___of___ them like to
of   to

walk. ___Both___ people go for
Both   By

a walk with the dog.

3. We have ___no___ money to
no   am

pay the food bill. He ___has___
him   has

money to buy us food.

4. We get water ___for___ the
not   for

man. The woman helps ___him___
him   in

walk to the table.

Review: pages 59–63

STUDENT OBJECTIVE
Review 20 new sight words in sentences and photos

ACTIVITIES
1. Comprehension: For *A*, ask: Where is the speaker working? Where is the store? For *B*, ask: Who

gets money? Who pays the brother? **2.** Point out that now students are reading several paragraphs. Ask how many paragraphs there are, and how they got the answer.

A. Look at the words in the word box.
Then read the sentences.
Write the word that completes each sentence.

1. I ___am___ working with people at a country store. A woman working with ___us___ has a family.

| us |
| am |

2. Her family ___has___ a home. She walked ___by___ it with me.

| has |
| by |

3. She likes ___her___ job at the store. She likes to work ___with___ people.

| with |
| her |

4. The store is ___in___ the country. ___We___ like to walk to work. Her dog walks with ___us___ to the store.

| We |
| in |
| us |

B. Read these paragraphs.
Underline the words in each paragraph that are in the word boxes.

Her family helps <u>at</u> home. The brother gets money for helping with the work. He gets money from the sisters. They pay <u>him</u> <u>to</u> work.

| to | at |
| him | |

The sisters <u>have</u> jobs at the food store. They are <u>not</u> at home. <u>Both of them</u> have cars to get to work.

Both	them
not	have
of	

The brother has <u>no</u> car. He uses the bus. He pays <u>for</u> the bus with the money he gets <u>from</u> the sisters.

| for | no |
| from | |

Practice:

STUDENT OBJECTIVE
Practice sight words in new contexts

ACTIVITY
After students complete *B*, have them reread the two sets of sentences that they did not write. Ask them to describe a photo that could go with each set.

at   am   from   him

**A. Read the sentences.
Write the new words.**

1. I **am** standing **at** the bus stop. ____am____ ____at____

   I **am** going to work. ____am____

   I **am** sick of going to work. ____am____

2. I **am** working for a boss. ____am____

   I get money **from him** for working. ____from____ ____him____

   I go home **from** work with **him**. ____from____ ____him____

3. I **am** going to the food store with **him**. ____am____ ____him____

   I **am** going **from** work. ____am____ ____from____

   I **am** going to buy food **at** the store for **him**. ____am____ ____at____ ____him____

**B. Read these sentences.
Write the sentences that go with the photo.**

1. The woman is looking at the car.
   The man is looking at the car.

2. She is looking at him.
   He is looking at her.

3. She is walking with him.
   I am walking with them.

   She is looking at him.

   He is looking at her.

Practice:

STUDENT OBJECTIVE
Practice sight words in new contexts

ACTIVITY
Phonics: Ask students which of the practice words have the same beginning sound. Ask them to tell you other words that begin with *b*.

both   by   of   them

A. Read the sentences.
Write the new words.

1. They are going **by** car. _____by_____

2. **Both of them** use the car to go to the store. __Both__ __of__ __them__

3. **Both of** us are going with **them**. __Both__ __of__ __them__

4. **Both** sisters have dogs. __Both__

5. **Both of them** walk the dogs **by** the water. __Both__ __of__ __them__ __by__

B. Read these sentences.
Write the sentence that goes with the photo.

1. People get bills, and people pay them.

2. Both people are sick, and the nurse helps them.

3. We go by car, and both of them go by bus.

4. Both dogs like walking by the water.

5. They work with both of the sisters.

6. Both of the homes are by work.

   People get bills, and people pay them.

Practice:

STUDENT OBJECTIVE
Practice sight words in new contexts

ACTIVITY
Phonics: Ask students which of the practice words have the same beginning sound. Ask them to tell you other words that begin with *w*.

we	us	not	with

A. Read the sentences. Write the new words.

1. **We** are sick in bed and can **not** go to work. ___We___ ___not___

   We are **not** well; we are at home. ___We___ ___not___

2. Are you working **with us**? ___with___ ___us___

   He is **not** working **with us**; he is helping the boss. ___not___ ___with___ ___us___

3. **We** can walk **with** him to the bus stop. ___We___ ___with___

   She can **not** walk **with us**; she is going by car. ___not___ ___with___ ___us___

B. Read these sentences. Write the sentences that go with the photo.

1. We are going to the bus stop.
   Can we use this bus to get to work?

2. She is not going with us.
   She is going to work in her car.

3. They can not go to work with us.
   They are walking with him.

   ___She is not going with us.___

   ___She is going to work in her car.___

Practice:

STUDENT OBJECTIVE
Practice sight words in new contexts

ACTIVITY
Phonics: Ask students which of the practice words have the same beginning sound. Ask them to tell you other words that begin with *h*.

have   no   has   in

A. Read the sentences. Write the new words.

1. I **have** **no** car keys with me. ___have___ ___no___

   She **has** the keys **in** her home. ___has___ ___in___

   I can not get **in** the car. ___in___

   She **has** to go home and get the keys. ___has___

2. **No**, I can not get **in** the water with you. ___No___ ___in___

   I **have** to go home and go to work. ___have___

   She **has** to go with me and help me with the job. ___has___

B. Read the sentences. Write the sentences that go with the photo.

1. The dog has her food.
   I have water for her.

2. She works in a store.
   He has no work.

3. The family has a home.
   The brother works in the home.

   The dog has her food.

   I have water for her.

Practice:

STUDENT OBJECTIVE
Practice sight words in new contexts

ACTIVITY
Comprehension: In *A* ask: Why is the speaker looking for someone? Why is the speaker buying a radio?

for   her   me   to

A. Read the sentences.
Write the new words.

1. I am looking **for her**; I have money for her. ___for___ ___her___

   She can use the money from **me to** pay **her** bills. ___me___ ___to___ ___her___

2. This zipper is **for me to** use. ___for___ ___me___ ___to___

   The quarters are **for her to** buy dog food. ___for___ ___her___ ___to___

3. Go **to** the store **for me** and get the food. ___to___ ___for___ ___me___

   I like her, and I am buying a radio **for her**. ___for___ ___her___

B. Read the sentences.
Write the sentences that go with the photo.

1. The boss pays me to work.
   I pay her to help me.

2. She uses her money to buy food.
   The food is for her family.

3. I use the money to pay the light bill.
   We use the lights to work at home.

   She uses her money to buy food.

   The food is for her family.

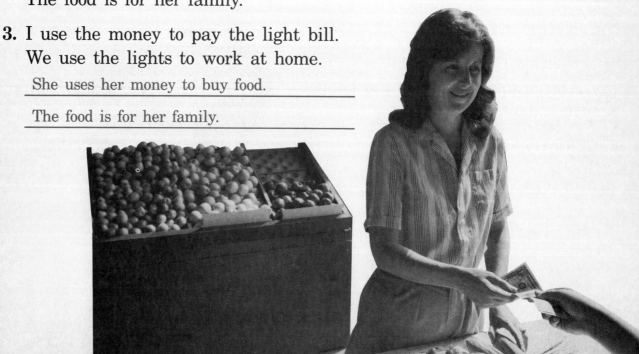

Review: pages 66-70

STUDENT OBJECTIVE

Review 20 practice words in sentences and photos

ACTIVITY

Ask students to pick one of the photos and make up a story about it, using the sentences provided as a starting point. Have students say what might have happened before the photo, and what might happen next. Write the students' story on the board. Read it to them and have them read after you in chorus.

Look at each photo.
Then read the sentences.
Write the word that completes each sentence.

1. _____Both_____ of us go for a walk.
   <u>Both</u>   <u>them</u>

   She can _____not_____ go with us.
   <u>her</u>   <u>not</u>

   _____We_____ walk the dog for her.
   <u>We</u>   <u>From</u>

2. They stand _____by_____ the van.
   <u>by</u>   <u>me</u>

   I _____am_____ not going with
   <u>of</u>   <u>am</u>
   them.

   I am going _____to_____ work.
   <u>to</u>   <u>me</u>

3. I _____have_____ her keys.
   <u>have</u>   <u>him</u>

   She is not _____at_____ home.
   <u>at</u>   <u>us</u>

   _____Her_____ dog is at home.
   <u>In</u>   <u>Her</u>

4. She _____has_____ a big table.
   <u>has</u>   <u>in</u>

   Her sisters work _____at_____ the
   <u>at</u>   <u>has</u>

   table. They work _____for_____ her.
   <u>for</u>   <u>have</u>

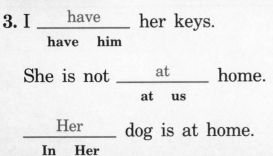

Review: pages 66–70

STUDENT OBJECTIVE	ACTIVITIES
Review 20 practice words in sentences and paragraphs	**1. Comprehension:** In *A*, ask: Where are the speakers going? What is the speaker buying? How will they

get home? In *B*, ask: Why does the family like the man? Why does the man help the family?
2. Dictation: Repeat the dictation activity outlined on p. 21, using the new words on pp. 66–70.

A. Look at the words in the word box.
Read the sentences.
Write the word that completes each sentence.

1. _____We_____ are going from work to the store. That man is going with ___us___. He is ___not___ going home.

We
not
us

2. In the store they ___have___ zippers. I looked ___at___ this zipper. I ___am___ buying it for her.

am
have
at

3. We can walk home ___from___ the store. You can go home with ___me___. The man can go home ___by___ bus.

me
from
by

B. Read these paragraphs.
Underline the words in each paragraph that are in the word boxes.

This man and I work in the city. Both of us walk home from work.

Both	from
of	us

We stop by the home of a sick family. The man has food for them. He pays the bills for them.

them	for
by	has

The family likes him. He is like a brother to the people in the family. He has no family in this city.

him	in
no	

Number Words:

STUDENT OBJECTIVES
Master the number words zero–five

TEACHING NOTE
Write the numbers 0–5 on the board; ask students to identify them. Then read each number word and listen to students read after you.

| zero | one | two | three | four | five |

A. Look at the photos.
Read the words and numbers.
Write the number word under the photo.

zero 0

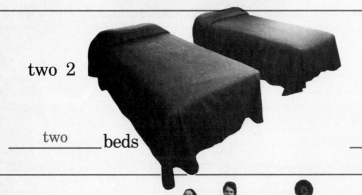

__zero__

one 1

_____one_____ home

two 2

_____two_____ beds

three 3

_____three_____ tables

four 4

_____four_____ people

five 5

_____five_____ lights

B. Draw a line from the number to the word.

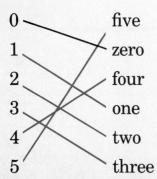

0 — five
1 — zero
2 — four
3 — one
4 — two
5 — three

C. Write the number words in order.

five   two   four
three   zero   one

zero one

two   three

four   five

Number Words:

STUDENT OBJECTIVES
Master the number words six–ten

TEACHING NOTES
1. Repeat the procedure on p. 73.
2. Tell students number words most often appear in newspaper articles and books. Read them examples.

six	seven	eight	nine	ten

A. Look at the photos.
Read the words and numbers.
Write the number word by the photo.

six 6

_____six_____ radios

seven 7

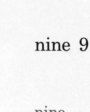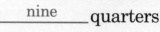

_____seven_____ keys

eight 8

_____eight_____ bills

nine 9

_____nine_____ quarters

ten 10

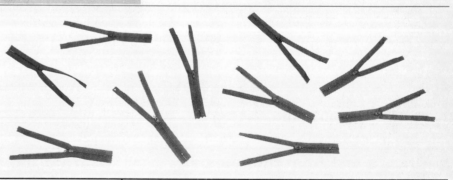

_____ten_____ zippers

B. Draw a line from the number to the word.

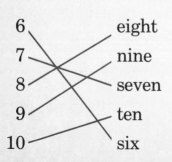

6   eight
7   nine
8   seven
9   ten
10   six

C. Write the number words in order.

eight   ten   nine
six   seven

six   seven _____

eight   nine _____

ten _____

Review: pages 73–74

STUDENT OBJECTIVE

Review number words one–ten

ACTIVITY

Explain that in C, students must count the total number of dots on each domino to get the correct answer. The number 10 will appear twice (6 + 4 and 5 + 5). After they complete this exercise, ask them to think of other combinations of dots that could appear on dominoes (3 + 4 = 7, 1 + 3 = 4).

A. Write the number that goes with the word.

eight __8__   seven __7__   one __1__   nine __9__

five __5__   six __6__   two __2__   zero __0__

four __4__   three __3__   ten __10__

B. Write the word that goes with the number.

3 __three__   6 __six__   0 __zero__

5 __five__   2 __two__   7 __seven__

1 __one__   4 __four__   8 __eight__

9 __nine__   10 __ten__

C. Count the dots.
Write the number and the number word under the dominoes.

__5__ __five__   __3__ __three__   __7__ __seven__

__1__ __one__   __10__ __ten__   __4__ __four__

__8__ __eight__   __0__ __zero__   __6__ __six__

__9__ __nine__   __10__ __ten__   __2__ __two__

Review: pages 73–74

STUDENT OBJECTIVE
Review number words one–ten

TEACHING NOTE
Before students start *B*, explain that they will have to do some simple arithmetic to get the answers.

REINFORCEMENT & PRACTICE
After students complete this unit, assign Unit 3 in the accompanying workbook, *Communication for Today*. The workbook provides additional reading and writing activities.

A. Read the words in the word box.
Write the number word next to the number.

0 __zero__   1 __one__   2 __two__

3 __three__   4 __four__   5 __five__

6 __six__   7 __seven__   8 __eight__

9 __nine__   10 __ten__

eight	one
six	nine
ten	four
five	zero
three	two
seven	

B. Read the number words in the word box.
Then read the story.
Write the number words that go with each sentence.

The Family

The family has two brothers and three sisters.

The family has __five__ people in it. The family has

__one__ home. The home has lights, tables, and radios.

One of the lights is by a table, and two of them are not.

The home has __three__ lights.

Four of the family work at a food store. Six people

work with the family at the store. __Ten__ people

work at the store. Eight of the people at the store

are well, and __two__ are sick.

one
Ten
three
two
five

Final Review

STUDENT OBJECTIVE

Review these *Book 1* skills: beginning consonant sounds and sight word vocabulary

TEACHING NOTES

In *A*, go over #1 with students. Encourage them to do the rest of the exercise independently. If they need help, tell them the words and ask for the beginning consonant. For example, in #2, say: The first word is *sick*. What letter does it start with? The second word is *sister*. What letter does it start with?

In *B*, encourage students to work together to see if they can think of some words without looking in their books.

A. Read the first word on each line.
The other words on the line start with the same sound.
Fill in the missing first letter for each word.

1. bus   <u>b</u>ed   <u>b</u>ig   <u>b</u>ills
2. sit   <u>s</u>ick   <u>s</u>ister
3. walk   <u>w</u>oman   <u>w</u>ater   <u>w</u>ith
4. family   <u>f</u>ood   <u>f</u>or
5. home   <u>h</u>elp   <u>h</u>im   <u>h</u>ave
6. car   <u>c</u>an   <u>c</u>ountry
7. me   <u>m</u>oney   <u>m</u>an
8. no   <u>n</u>urse   <u>n</u>ot   <u>n</u>ine

B. Below is a list of some of the words you learned in Unit 1.
Next to each word, write two or more words in this book that start with the same sound.
You can look through your book as you do this exercise.

1. bed   bus big bills boss
2. can   car country
3. food   family for
4. has   help home have
5. light   like look
6. man   money me
7. nurse   not no
8. sister   sick sit seven
9. table   to ten
10. walk   woman water work well

Story

STUDENT OBJECTIVE
Read and understand a two-page story containing most of the words in *Book 1*

TEACHING NOTES
1. Discuss what is going on in each photo.
2. Read the first paragraph aloud to students, and have them read after you in chorus. Repeat this procedure for each paragraph. Ask students to read the whole story through silently, then have them read it aloud in chorus.

The woman has a home in the city. She works in the city. The woman uses a city bus to get to her job. She works at a food store. She likes her job. She likes to go to work.

Her brother has no job. He is sick at home. The sister stops by to help him. She gets him food. She walks the dog for him.

Story

1. Comprehension: Begin with simple recall questions: Where does the sister work? How does she get there?

Then ask questions at a higher level: What will the brother do with the money he earns? Allow students to look back at the story, but encourage them to answer in their own words.

2. Follow-up: Have students make up the next page of the story. Write the story on the board, read it back to students, and have them read after you in chorus. Then have students read the whole story aloud again.

Today the brother is not sick. He walks the dog. He takes a bus to the store. He walks home.

A car is going by. The woman in the car stops at a light. She works at the store.

She has a job for him. The job pays big money. He likes the job and the money!

Word List

STUDENT OBJECTIVE

Practice classifying words

ACTIVITIES

1. Ask students to find the words in the list below that end in *s*. As students call out the words, write them on the board in 2 columns: plural words (beds, bills) and singular words (bus, boss). Point out that not every word that ends in *s* means more than one.
2. Ask students to make 3 lists of words: names of objects, names of people (man, sister, etc.), and action words. Guide them to put words from these lists together to make short sentences.

Below is a list of the 93 base words (131 with common endings) in Book 1 of *Reading for Today*. These words will be reviewed in later books. The numeral following each word refers to the page on which the word is introduced to the students.

A a 22
am 62
an 45
and 46
are 47
at 62

B bed 5
beds 73
big 18
bill 49
bills 40
boss 40
both 63
brother 30
brothers 64
bus 38
buy 26
buying 43
buys 28
by 61

C can 20
car 5
cars 35
city 38
country 30

D dog 6
dogs 28

E eight 74

F family 32
five 73
food 6
for 59
four 73
from 61

G get 36
gets 43

go 7

H has 59
have 62
he 46
help 32
helped 34
helping 42
helps 43
her 60
him 60
home 7
homes 28

I I 48
in 63
is 47
it 49

J job 8
jobs 65

K key 8
keys 28

L light 9
lights 70
like 38
likes 46
look 32
looked 34
looking 42
looks 35

M man 18
me 61
money 9

N nine 74
no 63
not 62
nurse 11

O of 63
one 73

P pay 38
paying 42
pays 49
people 11

Qu quarter 12
quarters 63

R radio 12
radios 28
run 18
runs 22

S seven 74
she 46
sick 13
sister 30
sisters 63
sit 18
sits 22
six 74
stand 18
standing 47
stands 22
stop 20
stops 22
store 38

T table 13
tables 28
ten 74
that 49
the 45
them 60
they 48
this 49
three 73
to 60
two 73

U us 59
use 24
uses 28

V van 14

W walk 24
walked 34
walking 42
walks 29
was 47
water 14
we 61
well 36
with 59
woman 24
work 30
worked 34
working 42
works 35

Y yell 15
yelled 34
yelling 42
yells 29
you 48

Z zero 73
zipper 15
zippers 63

BLACKFEET
INDIAN STORIES

BY

GEORGE BIRD GRINNELL

AUTHOR OF

"BLACKFEET LODGE TALES," "TRAILS OF THE PATHFINDERS," ETC.

FACSIMILE EDITION

APPLEWOOD BOOKS

DISTRIBUTED BY THE GLOBE PEQUOT PRESS

MAY '95

: published in 1913.

ISBN: 1-55709-201-X

10 9 8 7 6 5 4 3 2 1

Library of Congress Cataloging-in-Publication Data
Grinnell, George Bird, 1849-1938.
    Blackfeet Indian stories / George Bird Grinnell. —
Facsimile ed.
        p.   cm.
    Originally published: New York: Scribner, 1913.
    ISBN 1-55709-201-X : $10.95
    Siksika Indians—Legends.   I. Title.
E99.S54G8   1993
813' .52—dc20   92-40295
                                              CIP